THE SIMPLE HOME

CHARLES KEELER AT "THE STUDIO", CLAREMONT HILLS, BERKELEY.
PHOTOGRAPH BY S. V. WEBB, CIRCA 1909.

THE SIMPLE HOME

CHARLES KEELER

WITH A NEW INTRODUCTION
BY DIMITRI SHIPOUNOFF

➔

Peregrine Smith, Inc.
SANTA BARBARA AND SALT LAKE CITY

1979

Library of Congress Cataloging in Publication Data

Keeler, Charles Augustus, 1871–1937.
    The simple home.

    Reprint of the 1904 ed. published by P. Elder,
San Francisco.
    1. Architecture, Domestic.   I.   Title.
NA7120.K3   1979   728.3   79-13372
ISBN 0-87905-057-8

Introduction copyright © 1979 by Peregrine Smith, Inc.

Manufactured in the United States of America.

DEDICATED
TO MY FRIEND AND COUNSELOR
BERNARD R. MAYBECK

BERNARD MAYBECK IN WORK SMOCK AT HIS STUDIO. LIONEL BERRYHILL PHOTOGRAPH.

INTRODUCTION

I

The architectural development of the unique San Francisco Bay Region style left perhaps its most important literary legacy in Charles Keeler's little book *The Simple Home*. This book, dedicated to the architect Bernard Maybeck, was largely a polemic against the architectural shams and gingerbread of the Victorian age, and a paean to "a simpler, a truer, a more vital art expression" then taking place in California. Charles Keeler, a Berkeley poet, naturalist, and self-appointed policeman of the arts wrote on architecture from the standpoint of a layman. As Maybeck's first private commission in 1895, Keeler's house at Highland Place helped set an idealogical precedent for a new kind of architecture in north Berkeley. Keeler's subscription to this idealogy was partly a product of his experience of living in such a home. In initiating the formation of the Hillside Club, he urged his future neighbors to build houses in a style that would be compatible with his own. *The Simple Home* was written in 1904, during his presidency of the Hillside Club. As President from 1903-05, he extended the organization's purview to include the greater Berkeley hills, in an effort to protect them from shoddy housing development. Bernard Maybeck became the club's idol, Charles Keeler its high priest, and *The Simple Home* naturally became its bible.

INTRODUCTION

Keeler began to envision an aesthetic utopian community whose lifestyle would embody the ideals of the Arts and Crafts movement—a movement lately imported from England and flourishing in California's virgin land. As spokesman for the Hillside Club, he was sensitive to the simple, hand-made architectural style of that movement and fostered the works of its adherents. Keeler's enthusiasm and eloquence converted many prominent citizens and not only shaped the Berkeley environment, but helped to create what has since been called the Bay Region tradition of architecture—an architecture exemplified by the works of Bernard Maybeck, Ernest Coxhead, A.C. Schweinfurth, Julia Morgan, and others.

The Simple Home articulated the Hillside Club's ideals of architecture and landscape planning. The book's sober architectural polemics were paralleled as well by social comment on the American middle class, a class which had become "the natural outgrowth of a prosperous democracy," a class of consumers who had shamefully disenfranchised themselves from the original conception of home. To the poet Charles Keeler, the home was hearthside, a place to come *home* to after a weary day of work, a "shelter for daydreams." The average modern American, he argued, had lost sight of the notion of home as shelter—his dwelling place became for him a dehumanized palace of machine-made ornament, "the makeshift of a shoddy age." Modern materialism had enslaved the average man to such a degree that he was left with little time to spend with his family. *The Simple Home* opted for a simpler standard of living, one which would leave more time for art and culture, more time for family, more time to live.

Although Keeler's social message was by no means a new

INTRODUCTION

one, his book became a welcomed regional contribution to an international protest and the West Coast's answer to Edith Wharton's *On the Decoration of Houses*. By 1904 his critical assessment of life in the Industrial Age was common ground for anyone familiar with the works of John Ruskin and William Morris. In the late 1890s, the popular magazines *Ladies' Home Journal* and *House Beautiful* began campaigning in favour of the small house untrammeled by the "inhumanity" of Machine Age bric-a-brac. After 1901, the articles in Gustav Stickley's *Craftsman* magazine brought the ideas of Morris and Ruskin to middle-class America and became a forum and showplace for the new American home-craftsmen. One wonders whether the Hillside Club's library carried a copy of another book which was published in 1901 by a French author with the same Christian name as the Berkeley poet—*The Simple Life* by Charles Wagner. Unlike Keeler, Mr. Wagner did not limit his discussions specifically to the field of architecture. His plea for simplicity was nonetheless a familiar one to the simple-lifers at the turn of the century:

> Our eyes are wounded by the crying spectacle of gaudy ornament, venal art, and senseless and graceless luxury. Wealth coupled with bad taste sometimes makes us regret that so much money is in circulation to provoke the creation of such a prodigality of horrors.[1]

Keeler's return to the simple life was not a return to Nautre, nor was it associated politically with Stickley's brand of "Socialism."[2] Keeler's distrust of the Machine age was non-political and did not lead him to suggest an anti-urban Utopia or a return to a pre-industrial agrarianism. In glorifying the ethos of the handicrafts, the romantic poet was also a modern man of science who did not mis-calculate the ultimate utility of machinery. Of all the arts, architecture was the most utilitarian and, for Keeler, the Queen Anne period in architecture was exemplary of man's misuse of machinery—machinery which had run amok in producing architectural excrescences which had no relationship to the real needs of the home-dweller. Before machinery could be used effectively, the craftsman had to be restored to his original integrity, producing work that was both useful and beautiful.

Borrowing from the principles of William Morris, *The Simple Home* more than implies that the whole gamut of physical environment should be a source of exhilirating pleasure; it should be a work of art from floor joist to picture frame. Again paraphrasing Morris, Keeler insists that all works of man are potential works of art when begun at home—that the existence of all the decorative arts emanantes from the mistress art of architecture. "Gradually the dweller in the simple home will come to ponder upon the meaning of art,... It will then become apparent how truly the home is the real art center."[3]

Keeler demands uncategorically that the architect of the simple home be an artist, his contribution being the most public of art forms. A house, after all, is only an incident in a landscape. The architect as artist must not detract from nature, but essentially group his notion of "house as shelter" with what is already there. In the city, the house stands as a mere detail in a neighbourhood and consequently has the ability to shape the lives of those that come in contact with it from without, as well as those who live within it. If the philosopher Gaston Bachelard describes the interior of the house as man's "first universe," so too might we conjecture that Keeler conceived

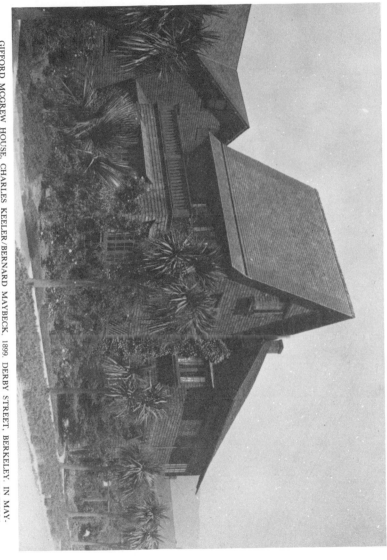

GIFFORD MCGREW HOUSE, CHARLES KEELER/BERNARD MAYBECK, 1899, DERBY STREET, BERKELEY, IN MAY-BECK'S ABSENCE, KEELER SUGGESTED A WORKABLE DESIGN FOR MCGREW'S HOUSE. THE HIGH-PITCHED "GOTHIC" ROOF IS REMINISCENT OF KEELER'S OWN HOUSE. PHOTOGRAPH CIRCA 1907. COURTESY OF ALLEN AND MARY WARNER.

BETA THETA PI FRATERNITY HOUSE, ERNEST COXHEAD, 1893. THIS HOUSE WAS AN EXAMPLE OF WHAT KEELER CONSIDERED THE HONEST USE OF STUCCO. PHOTOGRAPH CIRCA 1895. COURTESY OF MARION GORRILL.

of the garden as man's second universe, the neighbourhood his third, and so on.

The Hillside Club embraced Keeler's garden idealogy when it stated that "hillside architecture is landscape gardening around a few rooms for use in case of rain."[4] In their omnipresent use of the pergola, the new architects of the Bay Region had planned their houses to integrally include the garden as an extension of living space. Again, for Keeler, the landscape gardener too must be an artist, as his garden is only "nature controlled by art." Keeler urged his readers to take advantage of California's favorable climate, to get out into their gardens and meditate, relax, and enjoy.

A clear-cut case for the servantless household is never made in *The Simple Home.* Since the book addressed itself to the family of average means, the problem of dealing with a staff of servants in a wealthy household was not an issue. Almost all of the average households in Berkeley at the time of this writing had at least one servant—a houseboy or a nursemaid for the children. If servants are necessary, Keeler romantically assures us, their duties will no longer be "those of a drudge when elevated to the dignity of participation in family services and in the advancement and joy of home life." All art is the expression of pleasure in labor. The role of the woman preeminently falls within the context of this pleasure principle of labor, for she is the "High Priestess," as Keeler put it, "the one who has the supreme reward." If we are to understand him correctly, he seems to be saying that the woman's highest service to the simple home is the bearing of children; he implies further that higher education for the woman should serve no more than to make her an interesting mother to her children. It should be remembered that Charles Keeler was still a child of the Victorian age and was not fully prepared, within the limited scope of his book, to discuss the rights of women outside of the realm of the family.

Keeler limits his discussions to the residential architecture of the San Francisco Bay area, to Berkeley in particular. Certainly, he was best equipped to speak about Berkeley's worthy homes from the experience he shared with Maybeck in designing some of them. The reason for concentrating upon the Bay region alone is given rather unconvincingly when he explains that "here a quarter of the population of California is concentrated." Charles Keeler loved Berkeley so much that he seems to be straining at this point in an effort to resist the temptation of a Berkeley chauvinism. In his discretion, Berkeley is never mentioned in name and, unfortunately for architectural historians, his photographic illustrations of Berkeley houses (taken by his sister, Sarah Isley Keeler) are not identified and regrettably few in number. Unlike Keeler's other book productions, the binding and lay-out of the original edition of *The Simple Home* were calculatedly spare and undecorated. This presentation was presumably the suggestion of his wise publisher Paul Elder.

Like the simple home itself, Keeler's polemical style of writing is generally "quiet in effect, restrained in tone." Although *The Simple Home's* frequent effusiveness is characteristic of the poet who wrote it, its style never cheapens itself by employing the strident exhortations of a propaganda leaflet. The Policeman of the Arts, nonetheless, lays down the law where matters of taste are concerned, his qualification being that "it is better to convey a definite impression, even though it be a narrow one, rather than to be so broad that all concreteness vanishes in glittering generalities."

Keeler primarily advocated the use of wood for the building of the home. As his own home was built of that material, he was naturally prejudiced in favor of it. In speaking to the more sophisticated members of California's middle class, he extolls the virtues of unpainted wood as a natural and beautiful building material suitable for the Bay Region's mild climate; but moreover he recommends it out of economic considerations. A simple home could be honestly built with brick or stone, but the high cost of those materials could only be afforded by the wealthy.

Keeler allows the average man to content himself with wood. By the same token, the Greene brothers' over-indulgence in woodcraft is relegated to the wealthy purse. Keeler's discretion allows him not to identify the already-famous Volney C. Moody house, which was an expensive "simple home" built of clinker brick.[5] The charred brick, if one could afford it, was aesthetically advisable in building a more substantial house. It was the redwood shingle's textural counterpart in masonry.

In 1904, Keeler was still writing in the age of Berkeley's wooden houses. Stucco in residential buildings at this time had not gained its wide use of later years.[6] For the author of *The Simple Home,* the best examples of stucco construction in the Bay Region were to be found in the half-timbered homes of Willis Polk and Ernest Coxhead. The worst examples were the "sham stucco" buildings, the most offensive of which were the fake Mission style houses much in vogue in California. Keeler wrote, in a later article for *Architect and Engineer,* that stucco was an admirable material for the exterior of a house, "so long as it is used over wood confessedly as stucco, and not as an imitation of masonry." In that same article he concludes:

> Like other shams, it will be found out and discarded when men come to think more seriously of their work. Open timber-work and plaster is more satisfying because it is just what it professes to be."[7]

In *The Simple Home,* he dismisses sham stucco as unworthy for the home of any "honest man," but good enough as a temporary structure for a World's Fair. Ironically, one of his mentor's greatest architectural creations would be a masterpiece of chicken-wire and plaster—Maybeck's Palace of Fine Arts for the Panama Pacific Exposition of 1915.

Rather than giving well-defined architectural guidelines for the modest home, Keeler's book communicates more effectively as a philosophical framework for the life and spirit of its dwellers. In suggesting an architecture that came closest in touch with the life of man, Keeler took his cue from the Arts and Crafts builders and particularly from Bernard Maybeck who saw a new humanism in the models of a pre-industrial vernacular. Of Maybeck he wrote:

> He looked to the old Gothic builders for sincerity, directness and faith of his work...it called for better carpenter work and joinery, for craftsman furniture, hand-wrought fixtures, and simple, vital ornament. It was sometimes crude but always vital, sincere, picturesque. It was a new type of architecture harking back to the old, but with no straining for effect.[8]

Nowhere in *The Simple Home* is one style advocated over another. Although Florence Boynton's open-air Grecian temple was a departure from the popular redwood-shingle aesthetic, it was nevertheless in the spirit of what Charles Keeler and the Hillside Club sought after in a simple home. As President of the Hillside Club, Keeler issued a pamphlet urging prospective home builders who could not afford the services of an architect to consult the Club's collection of prints and books before deciding on a style. For general types of vernacular architecture, he recommended broadly that "the Swiss chalets, old English, old Nuremberg, old Italian, and old Spanish houses may well be studied for suggestion and inspiration."[9]

If an architect is affordable to the home builder, he must of necessity be a member of the "new school," one who looks upon his profession "not as a trade but as an art." The "new school" in north Berkeley also produced an impressive crop of non-architects, or owner-designers, whose efforts were heavily influenced by the Hillside Club's directives. Most of them were familiar with the "helpful hints for homebuilders" in Keeler's widely circulated booklet.

Keeler seems to be implying that there is a hierarchy of simple homes, ranging in quality from the crudest conceptions of an owner-designer to the grandest of bungalows by Greene and Greene. Since the advent of modern functionalism, one would tend to think of simplicity as the absence of ornament. The application of the word "simple" in describing some of the lavish cottages in Berkeley seems to be a contradiction in terms. From the functionalist's point of view, they were anything but "simple." Presumably, the quality of simplicity was not strained by elaborate craftsmanship. The ornamentation of the simple home was not applied for its own sake as it was by the Victorian builders, but was integrally a part of structure. Keeler felt that Maybeck, of all the Bay Region architects, was most faithful in emphasizing the basic structure of a house as ornament:

> ...his idea was to glorify the materials, not to hide them away as if in shame under paint and plaster. His ornament was found in structural emphasis. The timbers were exposed, the strength and character of the construction made the design.[10]

It is not enough to narrow the essence of Keeler's manifesto by merely explaining his notion of simplicity in terms of historical or cultural relativity. True enough, his house at Highland Place is simple in design when compared to a house in the Queen Anne mode and, in a matter of degree, the miner's shack is simpler still. Keeler's house and the miner's shack are both *honest shelters* and what they share most in common is the utility of fulfilling the basic needs of their dwellers. "Let the work be simple and genuine," Keeler says, "...let it be a genuine expression of the life which it is to environ." The design in both examples is an honest expression of the materials used in construction and an equally honest function of basic structure. If these guiding tenets are observed, the degree of ornamentation becomes only a rational expression of the individual taste of the maker.

Keeler's book supported an architecture that would also become a moral prescription for California living. It was Maybeck's contention that the Victorian style of architecture died because of its "dreadful absence of beauty."[11] To Keeler, utility was simplicity, and simplicity demanded beauty as an essential of its fulfillment. The absence of beauty in architecture exposed not only poor taste, but the moral degeneration of all the arts. The simple home was to be beautiful and its truth is found in Keeler's faint expression of religious idealism. This nascent idealism surfaced initially in the pre-

CHARLES AND LOUISE KEELER IN LIVING ROOM AT HIGHLAND PLACE HOUSE. PHOTOGRAPH CIRCA 1896, COURTESY OF KEELER FAMILY.

TREE-LINED STREETSCAPE OF DWIGHT WAY IN BERKELEY'S ARCADIAN VILLAGE DAYS, CIRCA 1899. TO THE RIGHT, THROUGH THE ELM TREES, IS THE STICK STYLE HOUSE THAT KEELER'S STEPFATHER PURCHASED SHORTLY AFTER HIS ARRIVAL IN BERKELEY. PHOTOGRAPH COURTESY OF MARION GORRILL.

INTRODUCTION

face to *The Simple Home* when he stated that "All the arts are modes of expressing the One Ideal...thus it happens that architecture, the most utilitarian of the arts, underlies all other expressions of the ideal..."[12] In his conclusion, he celebrates the family in terms of a secularized Christian ethos of *service inspired by love.* The simple home would be the salvation of the human race:

> We hear much in these days of race suicide, but the menace comes not from those who love their homes. It is only amongst those for whom the feverish pleasures of the world outweigh the simple joys of the hearthstone that this danger exists.

II

When Charles Keeler's family arrived in Berkeley in 1887, they found the place to be a provincial college town, an Arcadian village with no paved streets or sidewalks; boardwalks lined only a few commercial sectors. It was a dustbowl in the summer and a mire of mud in the winter. With the exception of a few fine examples of late Victorian homes, Berkeley's architecture was nothing out of the ordinary. Duplicates of these white-painted clapboard structures could be found anywhere along the California coast, or almost anywhere in the rest of the country for that matter. The commonplace in Berkeley was offset by the magnificent color of the surrounding natural landscape and the town's penchant for lavish gardening. Although Berkeley's architecture was comparatively plain, its townscape in the area north of the University grounds began acquiring an unusual ambience, an ambience that would become legendary by the turn of the century. In a later reminiscence, Keeler described those early days:

But Berkeley was a remarkable village even in those days because of the people of culture attracted here by the University, and there were many delightful homes set in ample gardens with exotic flowers and near-by orchards. Only the architecture of the period was for the most part in the prevailing poor taste of the late Queen Anne period.[13]

In 1887, a challenge to this parochial trend in California came in the form of the Reverend Joseph Worcester's unpainted shingle houses on Russian Hill in San Francisco. In fact, as far back as 1876, the Piedmont Hills south of Berkeley prematurely witnessed the genesis of the Bay Region shingle style in a simple cottage which he had designed and built there for himself. Nearly a decade would pass before Bernard Maybeck would match and surpass Worcester's example with his unprecedented design for Charles Keeler's home in Berkeley. Keeler's family, for the time being, contented themselves with the purchase of a large Stick style house on Dwight Way in Berkeley, which was, in its day, an impressive residential creation by the eminent University architect, Clinton Day.

Bernard Maybeck arrived in San Francisco in 1890. The New York-born Maybeck had received his formal training in architecture from The Ecole des Beaux Arts in Paris. After graduation, he acquired field training in architecture on the East coast. Eventually, he came West via Kansas. He found employment in San Francisco as a designer and salesman for the Charles M. Plum Company, a firm which supplied custom interiors and furnishings to a well-heeled clientel.[14] During his service for that company, he and his wife, Annie White Maybeck, took up lodging in Oakland across the Bay. While there, he surely must have had an opportunity to visit Reverend Worcester's cottage retreat in the neighboring Piedmont

Hills. In a later memoir, Keeler describes this visit during Maybeck's residence in Oakland to have been "an experience that profoundly affected his whole artistic outlook."[15] Allowing for a dram of regional chauvinism and a dash of romantic speculation on Keeler's part we can assume that the sophisticated Maybeck found a source of reference, if not a "revelation" in Worcester's simple board and batten treatment of the cottage interior. Maybeck's innovations were the product of his native curiosity, his ability to absorb and successfully assimilate all of the architectural influences around him. If not in Worcester's prototype, the Bay Region tradition of architecture may very well have found its vestigial roots in the early California farm house or miner's shack. Slowly, and with humble offerings at its outset, a movement toward a more vital architectural expression began taking place.

Keeler's interest in architecture was born when he made the acquaintance of Bernard Maybeck in 1891. Keeler was then working in San Francisco at the California Academy of Science while Maybeck was still working for the Plum Company. Keeler's work at the Academy required him to commute back and forth from Berkeley on the ferry. On one of his trips across the Bay he chanced to meet another commuter.

> I cannot remember who introduced us, if indeed anyone did, but presently we began to meet and converse on the ferry...for a long time after those ferry boat conversations began, I did not know the name of my chance friend. I do not recall when I first learned that he was not Italian, and that his name was Maybeck.[16]

The older Maybeck took a fancy to this plucky young man who looked for all the world to be a romantic poet with his cape and gold-tipped cane. Over the next year, the two men would meet often and discuss the greater events of the day in the world of art. Perhaps the architect was already drawing plans in his mind for the home he wished to build for this young poet, as he one day offered Keeler his services. Keeler protested that he was not yet prepared to build. "Well," Maybeck persisted, "you may change your mind. If you do, let me know. I want to build a home for you."

In the meantime, Maybeck had left the Plum Company and secured a position as an architectural draftsman with the San Francisco firm of A. Page Brown in 1892. He had also moved from his apartment in Oakland to Berryman Street in Berkeley, where he began building a home for himself. This first residential effort of Maybeck's was in all respects handmade and, in its honest approach to the handicrafts, it became his first "simple home." Keeler was impressed by this realization of Maybeck's thoughts, and it convinced him to have his own home built.

It was not until 1895 that Keeler finally accepted his friend's offer and signed on as Maybeck's first client. They decided to build on a lot that Keeler had purchased some years earlier. It was located in an undeveloped area north-east of Charter Rock on a rise above a small creek which coursed through Blackberry Canyon. The whole of San Francisco Bay could be seen from there and the surrounds were sheltered by ancient California live oaks.

Maybeck divined the landscape and built a house which rose in elevation with the gentle slope and arranged its floor plan with the rhythm of nature—a site-sensitive solution in radical opposition to the rigid grid system by which the houses in the rest of the town were platted. The resulting structure

BERNARD MAYBECK'S HOUSE FOR CHARLES KEELER (1895), SOUTHERN ELEVATION. A DECADE OR SO HAD ALLOWED THE HOUSE TO SETTLE INTO NATURE. KEELER AND HIS CHILDREN ARE PICTURED IN THE GARDEN. PHOTOGRAPH CIRCA 1907, COURTESY OF KEELER FAMILY.

THE HIGHLAND PLACE "COMMUNE." FROM LEFT TO RIGHT: HOUSES FOR WILLISTON W. DAVIS, 1897 (DESTROYED), CHARLES A. KEELER, 1895, WILLIAM P. RIEGER, 1899 (DESTROYED), AND LAURA G. HALL, 1896 (DESTROYED). RIDGE ROAD AT HIGHLAND PLACE. THIS GROUP OF HOUSES BY BERNARD MAYBECK CREATED A MODEL OF ARCHITECTURAL STYLE AND NEIGHBORHOOD PLANNING. PHOTOGRAPH CIRCA 1900, COURTESY OF KENNETH CARDWELL, C.E.D. DOCUMENTS AT U.C. BERKELEY.

cut the sky-line with a cluster of three steep-hipped peaks, bearing some resemblance to the roofs of Eastern European farm houses, but curving at their eaves in subtle mimicry of the pagoda. One was immediately reminded of a similar roof line in the Japanese Tea House in Golden Gate Park, a remainder of San Francisco's Mid-Winter Fair of 1893. "The result was a house of redwood within and without, with all the construction exposed, left in the natural mill-surface finish on the inside and shingled on the outside."[18] The house caused a sensation as it was a revolutionary architectural venture and quite a curiosity. In her diary entry for October, 1895, Louise Keeler recalled: "Mrs. Wilks was wonderfully enthusiastic over the house yesterday saying she didn't know when she had seen a house that so well pleased her—in which she saw not one thing to alter."

We do not know how highly to regard that neighbor's opinion, but undoubtedly there were other ladies among the curious townsfolk who thought the naked redwood to be a trifle vulgar. Years later Maybeck enjoyed telling the story of two old ladies commenting on one of John Galen Howard's houses: " 'Who lives in that funny house?' one asked the other. 'Oh,' exclaimed her companion, 'that's the house of Mr. Maybeck. He's the architect that plans all those freak houses, you know.' "[19] Others, however, were much impressed by Keeler's "freak house" for it represented to them the ultimate vanguard of modern taste.

As soon as the house was finished, Keeler began to worry that others, less sensitive in their approach to the landscape, would "come and build stupid white-painted boxes all around" him. Keeler, the inveterate proselytizer, began a

[xxi]

campaign in favor of a cohesive neighborhood designed in the idiom of Maybeck's vision. He almost describes himself as having been invested with a tablet of law to go as a missionary among the Philistines and preach the gospel of "the simple home." And the enterprising Maybeck lost no time in promoting his own services with or without his zealous client's advertisement.

By 1900, the neighborhood at Highland Place had realised a "commune" of Maybeck-designed houses grouped in harmony with Keeler's. Much was made of north Berkeley's hillside homes. Convenient literary parallels were drawn. Anna Pratt Simpson, reporting for *The San Francisco Chronicle* in 1904, felt that her faith in humankind was renewed in her ramblings north of the University grounds. She eulogized a "my field is my neighbor's field" philosophy:

> ...When you discover that all the latch-strings of the hillside homes are, in very truth, on the outside, you will have forgotten the charmingly futile, but ideal and honest efforts of the Concord people and their friends, if you do not feel that the spirit of Brook Farm broods over the hillside community.[20]

The University of California at Berkeley began attracting the East Coast's more adventurous intellectual elite. These "Concord people" came and settled in the neighborhoods closest to the University, which had already become a prodigious cultural beacon by the early 1890s. In 1896, the philanthropist Phoebe Apperson Hearst sponsored an international competition for a comprehensive University plan upon the suggestion of Bernard Maybeck. As well as building "rustic" middle-class homes for professors and their families, Maybeck, another Easterner, was also envisioning for Berkeley the monumental architecture of the Beaux Arts. "Westward the course of empire takes its way," and California became a new Greece with Berkeley her Athens, seat of higher learning. "The Athens of the Pacific" would dramatize her neo-Grecian fantasies in 1903 with the dedication of her open-air Greek Theatre on the University campus.

The University's rapid expansion created a need for professional people, professors, and deserving young men of letters. Along with them came also their camp-followers: the artists and poets, and the lumpen intelligentsia that most campus communities are heir to. These were the very "Philistines" from whom Keeler would meet little resistance in agitating for a modern California architecture. The most sophisticated of these men and women had arrived in Berkeley already armed with a discriminating, although as yet ungalvanized, taste in art; the Eastern examples of H.H. Richardson's shingle architecture were not unknown to them. They were well acquainted with the works of the landscape planner Frederick Law Olmstead in America, and William Morris, the foremost exponent of the Arts and Crafts movement in England. Berkeley's shingle-style homes were "built by intellectuals, not essentially people endowed with genius but the California variety of intellectual, productive... even folksy in his attitudes toward family and the good life."[21]

The cultural dictates of the new Athens at Berkeley nurtured a certain naive sense of "Art for Art's sake." The Bay Region's decorative style of painting was typified by the work of Arthur and Lucia Mathews, whose canvases would picture dryads dancing around California live-oaks, the Mediterranean's azure was the Pacific's blue. William Keith glorified the natural beauty of the Berkeley hills in his somber pastorals.

INTRODUCTION

North Berkeley was unspoiled and her young citizenry was innocent in its quest for a higher civilization. The lumber industry's unlimited supply of redwood allowed the professor of modest means to lavishly use this material in building an inexpensive Craftsman home. The same men who later decried the abuse of nature through the organs of The Save the Redwoods League (1919) inadvertently supported the very industry they railed against.

The ambience of the new Athens encouraged a healthy interest in natural foods and hiking. The Berkeleyans William Keith and Charles Keeler were both members of the fledgling Sierra Club and attended the summer encampments at the Bohemian Grove. Maybeck was a vegetarian. Keeler advocated jogging, or "running around the block," as it was called in those days. Before embarking on a world-wide poetry reading tour in 1910, he instructed those left in charge of the health and welfare of his three children to give them rub-downs with rock salt and corn meal, followed by an ice-cold shower.[22] North Berkeley's artistic colony was a health-oriented one and, for the most part, did not associate itself with San Francisco's brawling bohemia at Coppa's den. It was a puritanical society. While maintaining a genteel profile, turn-of-the-century Berkeley gave poetry readings, planted vegetable gardens, and slept on open-air "sleeping porches." George Wharton James credited Keeler with having introduced the first of these at Highland Place. Home-based arts and crafts guilds were organized in which furniture, pottery, and leather work were produced. The best products were displayed for sale in the showrooms of Vickery, Atkins, and Torrey in San Francisco—the worst examples were shared among self-congratulatory friends as the

KEELER IN GRECIAN ROBES DRAMATIZING THE FANTASIES OF THE "ATHENS OF THE PACIFIC."   PHOTOGRAPHS OF KEELER AND HIS FRIENDS IN COSTUME WERE USED AS STUDY PIECES FOR LOUISE KEELER'S BOOK ILLUSTRATIONS.   THIS PHOTOGRAPH WAS ONE OF A SERIES USED TO ILLUSTRATE KEELER'S   *A LIGHT THROUGH THE STORM* (1894). THE PHOTOGRAPHER IS POSSIBLY SARAH I. KEELER, WHO IS CREDITED FOR THE PICTURES OF CALIFORNIA HOMES IN *THE SIMPLE HOME.*

CHARLES C. BOYNTON HOUSE, "THE TEMPLE OF THE WINGS," PROJECT BEGUN BY B. R. MAYBECK/COMPLETED BY A. R. MONRO, 1912 (DESTROYED BY BERKELEY FIRE, 1923). VISIBLE IN THIS 1915 PHOTOGRAPH, TO THE REAR OF THE TEMPLE, IS THE "CAMP" WHICH MAYBECK BUILT FOR THE BOYNTONS TO LIVE IN WHILE THEIR HOME WAS UNDER CONSTRUCTION. PHOTOGRAPH COURTESY OF SÜLGWYNN BOYNTON QUITZOW.

crude, but honest, contributions of the "home" craftsman.

The new Athens took its advocation of the outdoors to extremes in Florence Treadwell Boynton's simple home. As an aesthete and follower of Isadora Duncan, she built a home in the open-air manner of the ancient Greeks. The entire roof of her home was supported by thirty-four Corinthian columns. Mrs. Boynton described this roof as "a pair of wings sheltering our nest" and her home was called the "Temple of the Wings." With the exception of a few conventionally enclosed rooms, the temple was open to the elements—in times of inclement weather sail-cloth drapes were unfurled from above and lashed to the columns with ropes. The origin of the popular misnomer "Temple of the Winds" is not a difficult one to fathom. Bare-footed they danced on radiantly heated concrete floors, under a roof with two circular skylights; the whole sweep of the town and Bay beyond it could be seen from their "sheltering nest" in the Berkeley hills.

Berkeley as Athens witnessed a population growth which emphasized a need for housing. Real estate agents were quick to sell and parcel land to those who sought to build their homes in the grassy hills and canyons north of the University. Environmentalists and guardians of taste feared for the natural beauty of these hills. In its discussions of art, life, and the simple home, Charles Keeler's Ruskin Club of 1896 inspired a group of north Berkeley women to protect this potentially endangered environment. In 1898 they formed the Hillside Club to that end.[23] The early meetings of the Hillside Club gathered in the evenings at Albert C. Schweinfurth's home-like church which had also served as the meeting place for the Ruskin Club. The meetings were also held in the homes of the

[xxv]

Club's members. After 1900, they met at the Hillside School. When they outgrew the schoolhouse, they commissioned Maybeck to build a permanent clubhouse in 1906. At its inception, the Hillside Club was an informal affair, a small citizen's action group whose membership was largely composed of people from the First Unitarian Church. Most of them came from the neighborhoods around Highland Place. They were a study group of women, whose primary objective was "to protect the hills of Berkeley from unsightly grading and the building of unsuitable and disfiguring houses." By and large, their campaign won over north Berkeley's newcomers with lectures of gentle persuasion. Early Hillside lore might suggest a more militant approach, when one imagines gangs of zealous women patrolling the neighborhoods well-armed with promotional pamphlets and umbrellas and upbraiding the unsuspecting offenders who were preparing to paint their clapboards white. One need only remember the Hillside Club's best known activist—Annie Maybeck, who rescued a tree from the hands of city workmen preparing to remove it, who commandeered a buckboard wagon and rode "like Paul Revere" down to the city hall to plead for its preservation.

The education that the Hillside Club offered began with its children. As well as preaching "art reform," Keeler often taught Sunday school at the Unitarian church—even the children were indoctrinated with the ideology of the "simple home!" The rest of the week these same children attended grammar school at the Hillside School House whose architecture had been entirely the inspiration of the Hillside Club. Their spacious classrooms were decorated with hanging plants and looked out onto airy verandahs whose roofs were supported by unpeeled redwood logs. In keeping with the spirit of nature their "blackboards" were green. "The entire building was of wood, with beamed ceiling, shingled outside, and finished inside with panellings of unstained Oregon pine. The fixtures were of hammered iron." It is little wonder, today, that the sons and daughters of the club's founders maintain a lifestyle which is still tempered by the lingering spirit of their cultural past.

The Club's membership had been bolstered by the wives of luminaries in the University community. Mrs. Charles Keeler, Mrs. Bernard Maybeck, and Mrs. John Galen Howard were prominent in their ranks. Unable to vote, these ladies were rendered politically ineffectual and had to rely on their husbands to take issue with the Trustees at City Hall. It was not until 1902 that the Club was reorganized to include men. A constitution was drafted in that same year; the Hillside Club was not incorporated until 1909.

The Honolulu *Sunday Advertiser* outlined the Hillside Club's objectives in an interview with its ex-President in 1911. On his world tour from 1910-11, Charles Keeler's poetry recitals were not without some comment on homemaking, the simple life, and a "return to the original method of making things by hand."

> ... The objective of the Club is to interest people ... to build their homes along certain approved artistic lines—low houses and broad lanais with plenty of yard room; trying to get people out of doors, getting them interested in flowers and gardens, and making the flowers and trees and gardens a more vital part of the home—getting closer to nature; working for open air schools; getting people to sleep on sleeping porches instead of in housed up rooms.[24]

[xxvii]

INTRODUCTION

As a civic improvement and development organization, the Hillside Club proposed a plan of co-operation for architectural improvement in other cities and towns in California. What direct influence they may have had on a statewide basis is difficult to determine. The local success with which Keeler and the Hillside Club met in broadcasting their "articles of faith" can be attributed to the intimacy of this small community to whom they addressed their appeal. In 1910, the journal *Architect and Engineer* gave tribute to the success of the Hillside Club and Keeler's simple home:

> When Berkeley's poet and author, Charles Keeler, organized the Hillside Club some five years ago to encourage the building of hillside cottages, he probably little realized how universally popular that type of home was destined to become. The then bare Berkeley hills are today dotted with picturesque bungalows, cottages and redwood shakes, the natural beauty of the hills affording a backdrop equal to any scheme wrought by the world's greatest landscape artist.[25]

III

The author of *The Simple Home* would have preferred that we remember him equally for his prolific contribution to California's regional poetry, for his scholarship in the fields of science, or for his directorship of the Berkeley Chamber of Commerce. In George Wharton James' biography of 1910, Charles Keeler was hailed as Scientist and Poet, one of California's most promising young men at the turn of the century.[26] His interest in architecture and his work with the Hillside Club were only incidental in a life so fully involved with the world of art. His whole life was marked by a magnetic attraction to the great men and women who foresaw a higher culture

HILLSIDE CLUB HOUSE, BERNARD MAYBECK, 1906 (DESTROYED BY BERKELEY FIRE, 1923). THIS HALF-TONE FROM A BERKELEY PROMOTIONAL PAMPHLET IS THE ONLY KNOWN PHOTOGRAPH OF THE ORIGINAL BUILDING (PUB-LISHED IN *WHO'S WHO IN BERKELEY*, GEORGE SUTCLIFFE, 1917).

HILLSIDE ELEMENTARY SCHOOLHOUSE, LOUIS STONE, 1900 (DESTROYED IN BERKELEY FIRE, 1923). THE SHINGLED HOME-LIKE ARCHITECTURE OF THIS PUBLIC BUILDING WAS ALMOST ENTIRELY THE INSPIRATION OF THE HILLSIDE CLUB. PHOTOGRAPH BY HUGO WEITZ, CIRCA 1901. COURTESY OF BERKELEY PUBLIC SCHOOL ARCHIVES.

at Berkeley. With all the friendships he shared with California's great ones, he has been seldom mentioned by local historians. In recent years, architectural historians have acknowledged Charles Keeler only in his connection with Bernard Maybeck.

Charles Augustus Keeler was born in Milwaukee, Wisconsin, on October 7, 1871. After he arrived with his family in Berkeley in 1887, he was soon assimilated into a convocation of pioneering Eastern intellectuals, who, like himself, had come to live in this small town at the edge of the Western frontier. He enrolled at the University of California in 1890. He was thrilled by the vast cultural opportunities offered him by the University and his preoccupation with wildlife was rewarded in his tramps through the hills and wooded canyons around the college campus.

Charles Keeler was open to anything California had to offer him. He was talented, progressive, in touch with California's nature, and receptive to an open marketplace of ideas at the University. He had already begun writing verses upon entering college. Although they were enthused by his poetic talents, his teachers were much more impressed by his early promise in the practical field of biological science. In 1891, his early scholarly interest in wildlife and his field experience with the U.S. Department of Agriculture was also impressive to the California Academy of Sciences in San Francisco.[27] He was hired by the Academy as the director of their natural history museum. As well as writing poetry, this ambitious young man was preparing an important ornithological treatise for publication while attending classes at the University. In 1893, the Academy published his monograph, *The Evolution of the Colors of North American Land Birds.*

[xxix]

INTRODUCTION

1893 was also the year that Charles Keeler married one of the daughters of the distinguished James S. Bunnell family of San Francisco. Keeler's wife, Louise Mapes Bunnell, had been a student of entomology at the University in Berkeley and was then pursuing her talents as an artist under the tutelage of the California landscape painter William Keith. In the following year, William Doxey, publisher of *The Lark,* introduced Keeler's first book of poetry. *A Light Through the Storm* was dedicated to William Keith and illustrated with Louise Keeler's drawings.

Charles Keeler was a decorous Victorian gentleman whose literary idealism flourished in a rather provincial Berkeley bohemia. His house was the gathering place for California's great cultural lions. It was not unusual for the Keeler household at Highland Place to receive a casual social visit from the poetess Ina Donna Coolbrith, or the editor of the magazine *Land of Sunshine,* Charles Fletcher Lummis. The young poet and his good friend William Keith would often take a saunter through the Berkeley hills or share a modest meal with the Reverend Joseph Worcester. Keeler was to be found at every literary salon or social function. His handsome six-foot frame was captured by every art photographer from Annie Brigman to Arnold Genthe. He was Berkeley's darling.

At best, Charles Keeler was a guardian of taste, a romantic intoxicated with the neo-Grecian fantasies of the "Athens of the Pacific." He was ever in the public eye, a flamboyant California dreamer, self-styled in the image of the European romantic poets. Unfortunately we have no recordings of his early theatrical oral presentations, which were reportedly spectacular. He sometimes recited in costume and read, as his daughter Eloise recalls, with a "voice that could fill stadiums." His interest in the masque and neo-Grecian lyric drama led him in later life to erect a simple outdoor amphitheatre at his last home in the Claremont hills of Berkeley. "The Live Oak" garden theatre, as he called it, was the setting for innumerable poetry readings and plays. His widely publicized pageant-play, *The Triumph of the Light, A California Mid-Winter Sun Mystery,* received enthusiastic acclaim when it was performed at Schweinfurth's shingled Unitarian church in 1905.

Charles Keeler, together with his artist help-mate, became the most vocal proponent of an indigenous Arts and Crafts movement in Berkeley. Their romantic and somewhat folksy mode of living at the turn of the century was exemplary of the "civilized" ideal for which *The Simple Home* was propaganda. Keeler owned and operated a publishing house, "The Sign of the Live Oak," from which issued a good number of his own poetry books and plays. Leading San Francisco bookmen, A.M. Robertson and Paul Elder, were also his publishers. His wife embellished these volumes of poetry, as well as his travel books, with her accomplished illustrations. It seems that Louise Keeler's Morris-inspired vignettes and book covers have better withstood the verdict of time than her husband's declamatory Victorian poesy. Keeler's literary craft, although generally competent and sometimes lyrically beautiful, suffered the lot of most Victorian poetry in its belabored archaic versification. One of the Keelers' best combined efforts was *A Season's Sowing* in 1899, a hand-illuminated book of poetry which affected an honest homemade "Kelmscott style" in its decoration; and, in its poetry, was somewhat reminiscent of William Blake. It was one of Berkeley's finest contributions to the Arts and Crafts movement in bookmaking.

The Berkeley poet, as author of *The Simple Home,* was more than the armchair critic of architecture that he appeared at a glance to be. As well as preaching the gospel of the "simple life," he was also its most avid practitioner. "In forming the Ruskin Club," Louise Keeler recalled, "in working in the Hillside Club, and in lecturing before teachers' institutes he has aimed to show the necessity of art in the home—in home-making, in home-deocration, and for a general spirit in our daily life." Keeler and his wife established a home-based Arts and Crafts guild from which they produced their own furniture for sale. Presumably, Charles executed the joinery and carving for Louise's design and decoration. With Maybeck's technical expertise, Keeler laid out the initial design for the home of his friend Gifford McGrew in 1899. After his wife's tragic death in 1907, a loss from which he never fully recovered, Keeler began building a writer's retreat in the Claremont hills. In the use of tinted stucco and open-beam construction, he tried his own hand at employing the principles which he had advocated in *The Simple Home.* It was a marvelous testimony to the Craftsman ideal—It became for him a rambling and un-tutored vindication of the handicrafts. Maybeck was respectfully amused by Keeler's "Studio" which was to take shape sporadically over a period of thirty years.

Keeler was always an adventurer and began serving his wanderlust with a trip around Cape Horn on the clipper ship *Charmer* in 1893. In 1900-01, he made a voyage with his family to the South Seas, visiting Tahiti, New Zealand, Australia, Samoa, and Hawaii. While on this voyage he worked as a reporter for the *San Francisco Chronicle,* sending back articles

A YOUNG MAN AMONG THE GREY BEARDS. CLOCKWISE: JOHN MUIR, WILLIAM KEITH, KEELER, FRANCIS BROWN (EDITOR OF THE *CHICAGO DIAL*), AND JOHN BURROUGHS. PHOTO TAKEN AT KEITH STUDIO IN BERKELEY, 1909. COURTESY KEELER FAMILY.

CHARLES KEELER'S "STUDIO," 1907, CLAREMONT HILLS, BERKELEY. THIS COTTAGE WAS DESIGNED AND BUILT BY CHARLES KEELER AFTER HIS WIFE'S DEATH IN 1907. ITS FLOORPLAN WAS INCORPORATED AROUND AN OUTCROPPING OF ROCK. PHOTOGRAPH BY EMILY PITCHFORD, CIRCA 1909. COURTESY OF KEELER FAMILY.

INTRODUCTION

about the natives of those lands, the most notable of which were his experiences among the Maoris of New Zealand. In 1910, he decided to leave his three children in the care of relatives and embark on a world-wide poetry reading tour which would take him to Europe and the Orient. The California poet was well-received by the English-speaking upper classes of those continents. He read before Queen Liliokalani of Hawaii and one of his poems was translated as a presentation to the Emperor of Japan. He was also a house guest of the Hindu poetess, Sarojini Naidu, in Hyderbad, India.

Borne by the momentum of his world tour, he returned to the States in 1912 and settled in New York City, where his craft was further tempered in a highly competitive literary circle. He was successful enough to have interested a New York publisher in his book of poems *The Victory* in 1916. After the first World War the Victorian poetry of Charles Keeler, George Sterling, and others like them, began to be outdistanced by a new school of poets: Robinson Jeffers and Robert Frost among them.

In 1917, Charles Keeler returned to Berkeley on the heels of a new era. He was a middle-aged representative of a provincial California culture whose geniuses had already begun to pass on from old age or despair—William Keith, John Muir, John Burroughs, Joaquin Miller, Ambrose Bierce, and Jack London had all died within the decade before 1920. Keeler's regional compatriot, George Sterling, would commit suicide in 1926. Keeler was caught between scene changes and the unencouraging prospects of supporting his two younger children in college.

In 1920, his reputation as civic leader in the Hillside Club days had secured for him the managing directorship of the Berkeley Chamber of Commerce, a post which he held until 1927. His new career was generally an active and innovative one and did much for Berkeley's civic betterment in his urging for parks and playgrounds within the city limits. Although the Jazz Age and Bauhaus had contributed to the eventual demise of the Arts and Crafts movement, the poet-director still dreamed of establishing an art colony in Berkeley. In 1921, he tried to interest Bernard Maybeck in designing the workshop buildings for a Berkeley Handicraft Colony. The colony would be a guild of craftsmen, an incorporation of hand weavers, metal smiths, book binders, leaded glass workers, printers, and leather workers. Apparently the venture never got beyond the planning stages. Toward the end of his directorship, he predicted with his usual romantic optimism that Berkeley would be one of the world's greatest art centers, a Utopia for poets, writers, playwrights, and composers of music.

The director of the Berkeley Chamber of Commerce still worked at maintaining his true calling as Berkeley's Poet. He and his second wife, the poetess Ormeida Harrison Curtis, whom he had married in 1921, were both active in the California Writer's Club. Keeler was president of this club from 1921-23. His literary production, although voluminous, was sadly un-marketable, as it had not adapted itself to the literary demands of the age. His one concession to the changing times was to write plays for radio. His serialized shows, "Skipper Brown's Yarns" and "The O'Flanagan Family," were immensely popular in the late '20s and early '30s.

As once a Unitarian Sunday school teacher and world traveler, Keeler was always fascinated by the religions of the world. In 1925, he defined his own spirituality in the book *An Epitome of Cosmic Religion*. Its message was an over-statement of the secularized Moralism which he had touched upon in *The Simple Home* and celebrated in all his poetry. His cosmic vision was no more than a broad-based universal religion similar to the Baha'i faith. Based on the teachings of his new religion, the inveterate clubman founded The First Berkeley Cosmic Society in that same year—it was his last attempt at realizing his utopian scheme for Berkeley. The Society's meetings were held at his garden amphitheatre and attracted a wide variety of Berkeley's spiritual aspirants. As a civic art's association, the Cosmic religion asked its members to "study, at least in a general and popular way, the researches of modern science, and to pursue the fine arts at least to the extent of cultivating a taste for good music, good poetry, good drama, good painting and sculpture, and good architecture." By 1930 the enthusiasm for Keeler's religion had dwindled. As Berkeley entered The Great Depression, her utopian dreams were set aside in favor of more immediate considerations. The Policeman of the Arts continued to dream.

On July 31, 1937, Charles Keeler died at his Studio in virtual obscurity. At his death the press gave him no more than a scanty farewell. The obituaries remembered him mostly for his service to the city of Berkeley in his capacity as managing director of its Chamber of Commerce. A street in the Berkeley hills was named after him. Belatedly, some twelve years after his passing, Hal Johnson, a writer for the *Berkeley Gazette*, honored "Berkeley's Forgotten Man" in a fitting biographical snippet for that paper.[28] This article in 1949 was occasioned by the Huntington Library's acquisition of a collection of

Keeler's correspondence. Two of the correspondents, the naturalists John Muir and John Burroughs, were numbered among his closest companions; the contents of their letters might have suggested Keeler's illustrious background in Berkeley's early days.

Keeler died disappointed by California's refusal to elect him her new Poet Laureate in 1933. He was also disappointed in the lack of interest for his First Berkeley Cosmic Society. His last great architectural dream for the Berkeley hills never came to pass:

> It is the dream of the founder of Cosmic Religion that a temple may be built in the Berkeley Hills.... Within such a temple would be the magic of modern lighting producing strangely beautiful effects falling upon moving water, stained glass designs, mural paintings symbolic of Cosmic Religion, sculpture and carvings. There would be organ music, chamber music, a symphony orchestra, and choir, dramatic pageants and allegories rendered.[29]

Much had changed, and more was changing. Keeler died wondering when the world would come to its senses.

—Dimitri Shipounoff

WALLEN W. MAYBECK HOUSE, DESIGNED BY BERNARD MAYBECK IN 1933, THIS HOUSE CONTINUED THE "SPIRIT" OF THE SIMPLE HOME ADVOCATED BY MAYBECK AND KEELER IN EARLIER DAYS. LIONEL BERRYHILL, PHOTOGRAPH.

WILLIAM W. UNDERHILL HOUSE, BERNARD MAYBECK, 1907 (DESTROYED IN BERKELEY FIRE, 1923). PHOTOGRAPH BY A STREET PHOTOGRAPHER, CIRCA 1910. COURTESY OF BERTHA S. UNDERHILL.

NOTES

1. Charles Wagner, *The Simple Life*. Translated from the French by Mary Louise Hendee. McClure, Phillips & Co., second edition, 1904, p. 141.

2. In providing an unalienating work ethic for the craftsman, Gustav Stickley's "socialism" was more a product of the philosophy of William Morris. As bourgeois purveyors to the Arts and Crafts movement, men like Stickley and Elbert Hubbard of Roycrofters set out to make "the simple life" a paying proposition. In all probability, their average workman could not afford to build a "Craftsman home" or buy a book from the Roycrofters Press. See: *The Craftsman, An Anthology,* ed. Barry Sanders. Peregrine Smith, Inc., 1978; and *The Arts and Crafts Movement in America 1876-1916,* ed. Robert Judson Clark, Princeton University Press, 1975.

3. Charles Keeler, *The Simple Home*. Paul Elder & Co. San Francisco, 1904, p. 52.

4. *Hillside Club Yearbook,* 1906-07. Bancroft Library, U.C. Berkeley.

5. The Dutch "corbie" gabled house of 1897 by Albert C. Schweinfurth is featured on page 8 of *The Simple Home*. As well as being peripherally a part of the Highland Place "commune," it was already famous in its own right. See *Architectural Review,* vol. 9, 1902; and *Sunset Magazine,* "Berkeley the Beautiful," December 1906.

6. A large number of Berkeley's wooden houses were destroyed in the great Berkeley fire of 1923; in re-building them, many of their owners were urged to avoid shingles and resort to stucco as a fire resistant material. After 1923, the exterior of Keeler's house at Highland Place was also remodeled in stucco by Maybeck for its new owner. An article in the *Oakland Tribune* for July 17, 1927, describes Maybeck's extensive remodeling of exterior and interior of the original Keeler house for Florence Babcock Hawkins.

7. Keeler, "Thoughts on Home-Building in California," *Architect and Engineer,* October 1905, vol. 11, no. 3, p. 21.

8. Keeler, "My Teacher Friends," p. 4. Unpublished manuscript in Keeler papers at Bancroft Library, U.C. Berkeley. Written about 1915, this manuscript was clearly an early draft for *Friends Bearing Torches,* a later work begun in 1934 and left unfinished at Keeler's death in 1937.

9. Keeler, "Hillside Club Suggestions for Berkeley Homes," p. 3. A 1905 Hillside Club pamphlet. Author's collection.

10. "My Teacher Friends," p. 4.

11. Kenneth H. Cardwell, *Bernard Maybeck—Artisan, Architect, Artist.* Peregrine Smith Inc., 1977, p. 21.

12. The meaning of the One Ideal is never fully developed in this writing. To the readers of *The Simple Home,* it suffices to understand it as a unifying creative principle. Keeler's semi-religious writings, most notably his *An Epitome of Cosmic Religion* (1925), define the One Ideal as "God, the perfect realization of the ideal of love, truth, and beauty."

13. Keeler, "Berkeley—Yesterday, Today, and Tomorrow." A pamphlet reprinted from an article for the *Berkeley Daily Gazette* of June 18, 1927.

14. Cardwell, *op. cit.,* p. 30. Refer to Cardwell's book for a more complete history of Maybeck's early career.

15. Keeler, *Friends Bearing Torches* (chap. "Bernard Maybeck, A Gothic Man in the Twentieth Century"), p. 226. An unpublished manuscript, Bancroft Library, U.C. Berkeley. The book was a collection of biographies of famous men whom Keeler had personally known. The chapters on Joseph Worcester, William Keith, and Charles Fletcher Lummis are of interest.

16. *Ibid.,* p. 223.

17. In *The Simple Home,* the illustration bearing the caption "The California Home in the Spirit of a Swiss Chalet" was Maybeck's Berryman Street house.

18. Keeler, "A Retrospection," p. 2. An invocation to The Berkeley Hillside Club Yearbook, 1907-08.

19. *Friends Bearing Torches,* p. 235. The house was Howard's own which he built on Ridge Road in 1903.

20. Anna Pratt Simpson, "Ideal Home-Making on a Berkeley Hillside." *San Francisco Chronicle,* Sunday supplement, August 14, 1904.

21. Robert W. Winter, "The Arroyo Culture," *California Design 1910.* California Design Publications, 1974, p. 14.

22. Information supplied in an interview with Eloise Keeler.

23. Keeler credits the idea for forming the Hillside Club to Mrs. Oscar Maurer. A strong case can be made for the important creative role of the women in north Berkeley. While the husbands were away earning a living in the City, the wives stayed at home and became, as Reyner Banham phrased it, "the true clients of the design process." The California woman as Hillside Clubber was liberated enough to make her mark on architecture.

24. *Sunday Advertiser,* Honolulu, Hawaii territory, September 10, 1911.

25. *Architect and Engineer,* vol. 19, no. 3, August, 1910, p. 83.

26. George Wharton James, "Charles Keeler, Scientist and Poet," *Heroes of California,* 1910. The only published detailed account of Keeler's early life.

27. In 1889, while still in Berkeley High School, Keeler was hired by the U.S. Department of Agriculture to study the migration of birds and mammals in the Lake Tahoe region. See James, "Charles Keeler, Scientist and Poet." As a leading ornithologist, Keeler joined the Harriman Scientific Expedition to Alaska in 1899. His future friends John Muir and John Burroughs were also members of the expedition.

28. Hal Johnson, "Berkeley's Forgotten Man," *Berkeley Daily Gazette,* May 9, 1949.

29. *An Epitome of Cosmic Religion,* p. 31.

CHRONOLOGICAL LIST OF
KEELER'S PUBLISHED WORKS

1893 — *Evolution of the Colors of North American Land Birds,* California Academy of Sciences, San Francisco.

1894 — *A Light Through the Storm,* William Doxey, San Francisco. A book of poetry illustrated with drawings by Louise Keeler.

1896 — *Promise of the Ages.* A book of poetry privately published.

1898 — *Southern California, Santa Fe, Los Angeles.* Illustrated by Louise Keeler. Reprinted in 1903 in *California and Back,* a book of practical information for travelers to the Pacific by C.A. Higgins, Doubleday, Page & Co., New York.

1898 — *A Berkeley Year,* chapter "Birds of Berkeley," reprinted from *Bird Notes Afield.* A collection of essays published by Woman's Auxiliary of First Unitarian Church, Berkeley.

1899 — *Birds Notes Afield,* Paul Elder & Morgan Shepard, San Francisco. Second revised edition 1907, Paul Elder & Co., San Francisco.

1899 — *A Season's Sowing,* A.M. Robertson, San Francisco. A book of poetry, illuminated and illustrated by Louise Keeler.

1900 — *The Harriman Alaska Expedition—Days Among Alaska Birds,* private publication.

1900 — *The Idylls of El Dorado,* A.M. Robertson, San Francisco. A book of poetry illustrated by Louise Keeler.

1902 — *Wayfarer's Songs of the Sea,* A.M. Robertson, San Francisco. A book of sea-faring songs, book cover by Louise Keeler.

1902 — *Tahiti the Golden,* Oceanic Steamship Company, San Francisco. Book cover by Louise Keeler.

INTRODUCTION

1902 — *San Francisco and Thereabout,* California Promotion Committee, San Francisco. Second revised edition 1906, A.M. Robertson, San Francisco. Book cover by Louise Keeler.

1904 — *Elfin Songs of Sunland,* The Sign of the Live Oak, Berkeley. A book of children's poetry. Book cover and illustrations by Louise Keeler.

1904 — *The Simple Home,* Paul Elder & Co., San Francisco.

1905 — *Triumph of the Light—A California Mid-Winter Sun Mystery,* a pageant-play, The Sign of the Live Oak, Berkeley.

1906 — *San Francisco Through Earthquake and Fire,* Paul Elder & Co., San Francisco.

1916 — *The Victory,* Laurence J. Gomme Co., New York. A book of poetry.

1919 — *Sequoia Sonnets,* Sign of the Live Oak, Berkeley. Illustrated by Merodine Keeler. A book of poetry.

1925 — *An Epitome of Cosmic Religion,* The Sign of the Live Oak, Berkeley.

1925 — Two poems published in *West Winds,* anthology of verse by members of the California's Writer's Club. Harr Wagner Co., San Francisco.

1939 — *Enchanted Treasure Island,* Professional Press, Berkeley. A book of poetry posthumously published by Ormeida Harrison Keeler.

SHINGLED HOUSE ON DWIGHT WAY AND PIEDMONT AVENUE (CIRCA 1898), ARCHITECT UNKNOWN. THE HOUSE HAS BEEN DIVIDED INTO STUDENT APARTMENTS.

THE SIMPLE HOME

BY

CHARLES KEELER

INTERIOR OF CHARLES KEELER'S "STUDIO." PHOTOGRAPH CIRCA 1909. COURTESY OF
KEELER FAMILY.

PREFACE

ALL the arts are modes of expressing the One Ideal;
but the ideal must be rooted in the soil of the real,
the practical, the utilitarian. Thus it happens
that architecture, the most utilitarian of the arts,
underlies all other expressions of the ideal; and of all
architecture, the designing of the home brings the artist
into closest touch with the life of man.

A movement toward a simpler, a truer, a more vital art
expression, is now taking place in California. It is a
movement which involves painters and poets, composers
and sculptors, and only lacks co-ordination to give it a significant influence upon modern life. One of the first steps
in this movement, it seems to me, should be to introduce
more widely the thought of the simple home — to emphasize
the gospel of the simple life, to scatter broadcast the faith
in simple beauty, to make prevalent the conviction that we
must *live* art before we can create it.

The following brief essays on "The Simple Home" are
written from the standpoint of a layman in architecture, and
are mainly intended to present, as graphically and suggest-
ively as such slight treatment enables, certain types of the simple home which may be infused with an art spirit. From such
homes, I fondly believe, will come not only the artists of the
future, but the public, whose faith and support are essential
to the permanence of art life in a community. — C. K.

[xlv]

TABLE OF CONTENTS

	PAGE
The Spirit of the Home - - - - - - -	1
The Garden - - - - - - - - -	7
The Building of the Home - - - - - - -	17
The Furnishing of the Home - - - - - -	38
Home Life - - - - - - - - - -	52

———

THE SPIRIT OF THE HOME

HOME life antedates the period of man by many evolutionary cycles. The aerie of the eagle, the woven cradle of the oriole, the tunneled retreat of the field mouse, all are homes in the truest sense. They are shelters from the world, where motherhood makes her eternal sacrifice, where family life and love find full expression, and where offspring are shielded and reared. The animal home differs primarily from the human home in its transitoriness. A few weeks or months suffice for the weaning of the litter or the fledging of the brood, and then the family scatters to the four winds. Even with primitive men the home is scarce more than a shelter for a brief interval in their nomadic life ; but with advancing culture, it becomes a more permanent affair. Groups of huts are clustered in a village which is the abiding-place of the tribe for years or generations. Then for the first time is developed an architecture.

Native architecture, like civilized architecture, is a natural growth. The nearest available material is worked into a shelter, and the tradition of form once established is handed down through generations. Thus the plains Indians of North America make their teepee in the form of a tent-shaped frame of poles covered with buffalo or deer hide ; the Pueblos of New Mexico build their fortified house of

stone or adobe and enter it by the roof; the Eskimo
construct a topek of sods with frame of whale-bone and
roof of walrus skin, or, in the far North, build their igloo
of snow masonry with tunneled entrance; the Tahitians
make beautiful bamboo fáres like baskets or bird-cages
roofed with thatched pandanus leaves; the wháre of the
New Zealand Maori is of marvelously carved wooden slabs
with intervening panels of bound grass and with thatched
roof of flax leaves. So, wherever we may go among
native tribes, a new type of architecture presents itself with
every new race, each using the materials at hand in a natural
and direct fashion to produce the needed shelter.

In the matter of privacy, it may be noted, the native is
far less exacting than the civilized man. Nearly all so-called
savage races are communistic in their lives. There may be
distinctions of class or caste, but the stranger is made welcome in the home circle, and the family is apt to be a large
and elastic group, comprising many distant and doubtful
relations, who live under one roof and in one apartment.
It is perhaps not too much to say that the dominant idea of
the native home is hospitality. In Tahiti the customary
salutation to a stranger, after the universal greeting,
"Iorana," is, "Come in and have something to eat." A
savage shares his food and home with the stranger quite as
a matter of course, never as a benefaction.

Something of this native spontaneous hospitality has
persisted in the traditions of California, where the mission
and ranch life of the Mexicans had an almost savage naïveté

in the matter of entertaining guests. In those simple days before the gringo came, a stranger could journey from San Diego to Sonoma and be sure of a welcome and hospitality wherever he chose to stop. Not only would a room and food be provided him, but upon his table, covered with a napkin, was a pile of uncounted silver known as guest money, from which he was to take what he needed to speed him on his way. We still have the tradition, but we have grown sophisticated since the coming of the Argonauts.

The ideal home is one in which the family may be most completely sheltered to develop in love, graciousness and individuality, and which is at the same time most accessible to friends, toward whom hospitality is as unconscious and spontaneous as it is abundant. Emerson says that the ornament of a house is the friends who frequent it.

In the conventional home, both the richness of family intercourse and the freedom of hospitality is restrained. A life hedged in with formality is like a plant stifled by surrounding weeds. Many people mistake formality for politeness, or even for good morals. There is a vast difference between good etiquette and right conduct. How depressing it is to go into a home where every act is punctuated with the formalism of polite society!

The home must suggest the life it is to encompass. The mere architecture and furnishings of the house do not make the man any more than do his clothes, but they certainly have an effect in modifying him. A large nature may rise above his environment and live in a dream world of his own fashioning, but most of us are mollusks after all, and are shaped and sized by the walls which we build about us. When we enter a room and see tawdry furniture, sham ornaments and vulgar daubs of pictures displayed, do we not feel convinced that the occupants of the home have a tawdry and vulgar streak in their natures? Or if all is cold and formal in architecture and furnishings, do we not instinctively nerve ourselves to meet the shock of a politely proper reception?

The average modern American home is a reflex in miniature of the life of the people. It is quickly made and lightly abandoned. If it were constructed like the Japanese house of bamboo and paper, or like a native hut of thatch, it might charm from its simplicity and lack of ostentation; or if, like the homes of our ancestors, it were made of mortised logs chinked with mud, it would have a rude dignity and inevitableness which would put it in harmony with the surrounding nature. But these things no longer satisfy. We must all have palaces to house us — petty makeshifts, to be sure, with imitation turrets, spires, porticos, corbels and elaborate bracket-work excrescences — palaces of crumbling plaster, with walls papered in gaudy patterns and carpets of insolent device — palaces furnished in cracking veneer, with marble mantels and elaborate chandeliers. It is a shoddy home, the makeshift of a shoddy age. It is the natural outgrowth of our prosperous democracy. Machinery has enabled us to manifold shams to a degree heretofore undreamed. We ornament our persons with imitation pearls

and diamonds ; we dress in felt wadding that, for a week or
two, looks like wool; we wear silk that tears at a touch,
and our homes are likewise adorned with imitations and
baubles. We botch our carpentering and trust to putty,
paint and paper to cover up the defects. On Sundays we
preach about the goodly apple rotten at the heart, and all
the week we make houses of veneer and stucco. Our
defense is that we do not expect to tarry long where we are
encamped, so why build for the grandchildren of the
stranger ?

Happily, a change is coming into our lives. Nowhere
in the country is it more marked than in California. From
small beginnings it has spread slowly at first, but soon with
added momentum. The thought of the simple life is being
worked out in the home. In the simple home all is quiet in
effect, restrained in tone, yet natural and joyous in its frank
use of unadorned material. Harmony of line and balance
of proportion is not obscured by meaningless ornamentation ; harmony of color is not marred by violent contrasts.
Much of the construction shows, and therefore good workmanship is required and the craft of the carpenter is restored
to its old-time dignity.

Blessed is he who lives in such a home and who makes
life conform to his surroundings, — who is hospitable not
only to friends, but to the sweet ministration of the elements, who holds abundant intercourse with sun and air,
with bird voices sounding from the shrubbery without and
human voices within singing their answer ! In such a home,

inspiring in its touch with art and books, glorified by mother love and child sunshine, may the human spirit grow in strength and grace to the fulness of years.

THE GARDEN

THE garden is the touch of nature which mediates between the seclusion of the home and the publicity of the street. It is nature controlled by art. In this assembling of trees, shrubbery, vines and flowers about the home, in this massing of greensward or beds of bloom, man is conjuring the beauties of nature into being at his very doorstep, and compelling them to refresh his soul with an ever-changing pageantry of life and color.

Unfortunately, in this workaday world, the possibility of the householder to be also a gardener is regulated by severe necessity. As men crowd together, the value of land increases, and so it is that in the heart of a large city only an enlightened public sentiment makes practicable the setting apart of areas where all may enjoy the redeeming grace of foliage and flowers. In proportion to the scattering of men is the extension of the garden possible, until the limit is reached in the lodge amid the wilderness, where the overpowering presence of nature makes the intrusion of an artificial garden an impertinence. In the village, then, the opportunities of the garden seem to be greatest.

But even the city home need not be wholly without the purifying influence of plants and flowers. Where houses are most congested and there is no land about the walls, one may resort to potted plants, and the streets may be decorated with palms or small trees in tubs or big terra-cotta pots. Vines may be planted in long wooden boxes, or, better still, in cement troughs against the sides of the house. If one objects to growing flowers in the rooms, little balconies or railed-in brackets may be built outside the windows for holding rows of potted plants. Hanging baskets containing vines or ferns are most effective on porches, while boxes of earth may stand upon upper balconies from which vines may grow and trail over the outer walls. A movement for the decoration, with geraniums and other plants and vines, of the residence district of the poor, would, I firmly believe, yield immediate returns in the advancement of culture.

Another expedient in the absence of land about the home is the roof garden. If this were sheltered from the prevailing wind with a wall or screen of glass, it would give the urbanite a miniature park where he could enjoy fresh air in seclusion.

But these devices are all makeshifts for the unfortunate ones who must live in the heart of a city. When a home is built in the town or country, the matter of a garden must be taken into consideration. Indeed, this should be studied even before the house is located on the land. Modern town lots are commonly cut up in long, narrow strips, so that by putting the house in the midst of a lot there will be a front and a back yard. This conventional arrangement has its advantages, although, as a rule, an unnecessary amount of space is wasted on the back yard, the chief utility of which

VOLNEY C. MOODY HOUSE, ARCHITECT ALBERT C. SCHWEINFURTH, 1897. THE HOUSE IS NOW A FRATERNITY. REMODELING IN THE 1950S BEREFT IT OF ITS DISTINCTIVE "COREIE" GABLES. LEROY AND VIRGINIA STREETS.

LILIAN BRIDGEMAN HOUSE, LILIAN BRIDGEMAN/BERNARD MAYBECK, 1899. ALTHOUGH
THE WORK HAS BEEN LARGELY ATTRIBUTED TO MAYBECK, WE CAN ASSUME THAT
THE INITIAL DESIGN CONCEPTION WAS BRIDGEMAN'S.   PHOTOGRAPH CIRCA 1900.
COURTESY OF LILLIAN DAVIES.

seems to be to afford room for the garbage barrel and for drying clothes. If a hint is taken from the compact method of clothes-drying practiced by the Chinese at their laundries, the land so often set apart for this purpose can be greatly restricted, thus correspondingly enlarging the garden. Two alternatives then remain — to place the house far back on the lot and have the garden all at the front, or to bring the house forward and have a small open plot in front and a retired garden in the rear.

Upon hillsides, if the streets are laid out in a rational manner to conform with the contour of the land, winding naturally up the slopes, the lots will of necessity be cut into all sorts of irregular shapes. This gives endless latitude in the placing of the houses upon the lots, so that unconventional groups of buildings may be set upon the landscape in the most picturesque fashion. But even when the lots are of the usual rectangular shape, much ingenuity may be exercised in the location of the house with reference to the garden. I have in mind one corner lot with a stream winding through it, shaded with venerable live-oaks. By putting the rear of the house on the property line of the side street, the front wall was close to the bank of the stream, and was approached by a simple brick bridge which led to the broad veranda about the entrance. This unusual location gave the effect of a large front garden, and made the stream the principal feature. A more conventional arrangement would have relegated this charming little watercourse to the back yard.

[9]

Whenever an entire block of homes can be studied in one plan, much more can be accomplished than by the customary method of each man for himself, regardless of the interests of his neighbors. For example, if the houses must be crowded together on lots of fifty-feet width, the garden space could be made to yield the utmost privacy by some such arrangement as the following: Suppose the houses to be set two or three feet back from the property line, leaving just room enough to plant vines and bright flowers along the front. If, then, a brick fire wall were erected on each fifty-foot division line, the houses could be built touching one another, and thus completely filling the block, save for the margin of flowers. By planning each house on three sides of a hollow square, with long, narrow rooms in wings extending lengthwise on the lots, each home would have an inner court, completely sheltered from neighbors, and with ample space behind it for a back yard. Or this scheme might be reversed by facing the hollow square to the street, in which case the court might be sheltered by a hedge or low wall. According to the former plan, the long front wall would perhaps appear somewhat monotonous, but it could be diversified by having generous passageways opening directly through the houses into the courts, and by the judicious use of open timber work and carving, if the houses were of wood, or of ornamental terra-cotta, if of brick. The continuous line of varied bloom next the sidewalk, with shade trees on the street, would relieve this scheme of any stiffness. I mention these devices merely to show that many interesting garden effects might be obtained by the exercise of more thought in the placing of the house, and especially by studying a group of structures in connection with their surrounding land.

Now, as to the garden itself: In the matter of architecture, two leading types appear to be in vogue in California, a northern and a southern, differentiated by an extreme or slight roof pitch. In considering the garden, two pronounced types are also encountered — the natural and formal — each of which is subject to two modes of treatment according to the character of vegetation used, whether this be predominantly indigenous or predominantly exotic.

By a natural garden I understand one that simulates, as nearly as may be, the charm of the wilderness, tamed and diversified for convenience and accessibility. A treatment of this sort demands very considerable stretches of land to produce a satisfactory result. The English parks are probably the finest examples of this type, which can hardly be successfully applied to town lots not over a hundred feet in width at most. In a district where the lots are happily laid out on a somewhat more generous plan, and especially where nature has not been already despoiled of all her charms, this form of garden may be developed to best advantage. If situated in the California Coast region, within the redwood belt, nothing could give greater sense of peace and charm than a grove of these noble trees varied with live-oaks, and with other native trees and shrubs growing in their shade, such as madroño and manzanita, sweet-scented shrub, wild currant, redbud and azalea, with wild-flowers peering from the leafy covert — the hound's tongue, baby-blue-eyes, shooting-star, fritillaria, eschscholtzia, and a host of others. About such a garden as this there is a purer sentiment, a more refined love of nature undefiled, than can be obtained by more artificial means; but such a garden needs room. Big trees, and especially such native evergreens as the red-wood and live-oak, take an unexpected amount of space, and if crowded together make the surroundings too dark and gloomy. On the California Coast there is need of all the sunlight that heaven bestows. Then, too, many people build their homes on the hillsides to enjoy the view. If numbers of large trees are set out about their homes, the outlook is soon obliterated, and the charm of far sweeps of bay and purple ranges is lost. It may be suggested that there are plenty of smaller native trees and shrubs that can be used, which will be adapted to a restricted plot of ground. Practically it will be found, it seems to me, that a garden thus limited to indigenous plants will prove rather dull in color and lacking in character. Without the woodsy effect of light and shadow, or the brilliance of cultivated flowers, the little patch of green will be apt to seem rather commonplace.

This brings me to the second treatment of the natural type of garden — the introduction of exotic plants into the scheme. The coast of California, as far north as the San Francisco Bay region, and the interior valleys for a hundred miles and more farther to the northward, have a climate of such temperateness that an extraordinary variety of exotics will thrive which, in less favored regions, would only live under glass. Bamboo, palms, dracænas, magnolias, oranges, bananas, and innumerable other fragrant or showy plants of New Zealand and Australia, of Africa, South America and the Indies, grow with the hardihood of natives. Among the trees most commonly introduced are such as the eucalypti, acacias, pittosporums, grevilias, and araucarias, but the number of successfully growing exotics is bewildering. Flowers which in colder climates must be carefully tended in pots, grow here like rank weeds, while vines that in more rugged localities develop a few timid sprays, shoot up here like Jack's beanstalk. An entire house may be embowered in a single rose vine. Geranium hedges may grow to a height of eight feet or more. It is a common sight to see hundreds of feet of stone wall so packed with the pink blossoms of the ivy-geranium that it appears like a continuous mass of bloom. The calla sends up its broad leaves and white cups as high as a man's head. The lemon verbena grows into a tree.

In the old-fashioned California gardens, advantage was taken of this prodigal growth, but without much study of arrangement. They were natural gardens of exotics, with curved paths, violet bordered, winding through the shrubbery. Often there was great incongruity in the assembling of plant forms, and the charm lay in the individual plants rather than in the ensemble.

Over against the natural garden, whether of indigenous or exotic plants, may be set by way of contrast, the formal

[13]

garden. The Italians are masters of this type of garden architecture, and it is to them that Californians may well turn for inspiration. A formal garden is one arranged according to an architectural plan, with terraces, pools, fountains and watercourses, out-of-door rooms, and some suggestions of architectural or sculptural adornment. It would be possible to design a formal garden exclusively or mainly of indigenous plants, but this would unnecessarily cramp the artist in his work. By having a choice of all the plants of the temperate zone, the landscape gardener is given limitless power of expression in his art. It is, of course, a prime essential to consider the effects of massing and grouping, the juxtaposition of plants that seem to belong together, and a due regard for harmony in color scheme.

Another type which may be studied by the Californians to great advantage is the Japanese garden. Conventional to a degree with which the Western mind cannot be expected to sympathize, it is, nevertheless, a miniature copy of nature made with that consummate æsthetic taste character-istic of the Japanese race. The garden as they conceive it must have its mimic mountains and lakes, its rivulets spanned by arching bridges, its special trees and stones, all prescribed and named according to certain stereotyped plans. But despite all this conservatism and conventionality, the details are free and graceful, with a completeness and subtlety of finish that makes the Western garden seem crude and commonplace by comparison. Their carved gates, patterned bamboo fences, stone lanterns, thatched summer-houses, and other ornamental accessories are original and graceful in every detail. Like the Italians, the Japanese make use of retired nooks and out-of-door rooms, while artificial watercourses are features of their gardens.

My desire in calling especial attention to these two types of gardens developed by races as widely sundered as the Italian and the Japanese, is not that we in California should imitate either, or make a vulgar mixture of the two, but, rather, by a careful study of both, to select those features which can be best adapted to our own life and landscape, so that a new and distinctive type of garden may be evolved here, based upon the best examples of foreign lands. As to the precise form which this new garden type of California should assume, it is perhaps premature to say, but one thing is vital, that at least a portion of the space should be sequestered from public view, forming a room walled in with growing things and yet giving free access to light and air. To accomplish this there must be hedges or vine-covered walls or trellises, with rustic benches and tables to make the garden habitable. If two or more of these bowers are planned, connected by sheltered paths, a center of interest for the development of the garden scheme will be at once available. My own preference for a garden for the simple home is a compromise between the natural and formal types — a compromise in which the carefully studied plan is concealed by a touch of careless grace that makes it appear as if nature had unconsciously made bowers and paths and sheltering hedges.

In the selection of plants there is one point which may be well kept in mind — to strive for a mass of bloom at all periods of the year. A little study of the seasons at which various species flower will enable one to have his garden a constant carnival of gay color. As the China lilies and snowdrops wane in midwinter, the iris puts forth its royal purple blossoms, followed by the tulips, the cannas, the geraniums and the roses (both of which latter are seldom entirely devoid of blossoms). In midsummer there are eschscholtzias, poppies, hollyhocks, sweet peas and marigolds, while chrysanthemums bloom in the autumn and early winter. These are but the slightest hints of the way in which a study of the floral procession of the seasons makes it possible to keep the garden aglow with color at all seasons of the year.

Let us, then, by all means, make the most of our gardens, studying them as an art, — the extension of architecture into the domain of life and light. Let us have gardens wherein we can assemble for play or where we may sit in seclusion at work ; gardens that will exhilarate our souls by the harmony and glory of pure and brilliant color, that will nourish our fancy with suggestions of romance as we sit in the shadow of the palm and listen to the whisper of rustling bamboo ; gardens that will bring nature to our homes and chasten our lives by contact with the purity of the great Earth Mother.

IN THE JAPANESE GARDEN AT GOLDEN GATE PARK.

BERNARD MAYBECK STUDIO. PHOTOGRAPH BY LIONEL BERRYHILL.

THE BUILDING OF THE HOME

HOME making is one of the sacred tasks of life, for the home is the family temple, consecrated to the service of parents and offspring. As the strength of the state is founded upon family life, so is the strength of society based upon the home. The building of the home should be an event of profound importance. It should be with man as it is with the birds, the culminating event after courtship and marriage, upon which all the loving thought and energy of the bridal pair is bestowed. How often in our modern American life do we find a far different procedure! The real estate agent and the investor confer, and as a result we have rows of houses put up to sell to shiftless home seekers who are too indifferent to think out their own needs, and helplessly take what has been built for the trade. The taint of commercialism is over these homes, and all too often the life within them is shallow and artificial.

The building of houses is an art, not a trade, and therefore it is needful that when those who are to occupy the home have thought out their needs, they should let an artist create out of their disjointed ideas an artistic whole. So apparent is this that it seems but an idle truism, yet comparatively few realize its full significance. It is not enough for a boss carpenter or a contractor to style himself

[17]

an architect and hang out his shingle. We must demand of our architect that he be a real creative artist — that he understand form and proportion, that he be a man of taste and originality, that he appreciate not merely the general types, but the inner spirit of the architecture of other peoples and other ideals of culture. Such a man will sublimate our crude and imperfect conception of the home and make of it a vital expression. Such a home will not merely fit us, but will be like the clothes of a growing child, loose enough to allow us to expand to its full idea, and with seams which can be let out as the experience of years enlarges our ideals.

It has often been pointed out that all sound art is an expression springing from the nature which environs it. Its principles may have been imported from afar, but the application of those principles must be native. A home, for example, must be adapted to the climate, the landscape and the life in which it is to serve its part. In New England we must have New England homes; in Alabama, Alabama homes, and in California, California homes. We cannot import the one bodily into the other surroundings without introducing jarring notes, although there is a certain quality in architecture which is racial and temperamental rather than climatic, — a quality not to be ignored or slighted.

Even such a designation as a California home is too inclusive, for between the climate and scenery of San Diego and Mendocino Counties there is as wide a diversity as between New England and Alabama. In the following discussion, much will be of general application regardless of climate or landscape, but those points in which environment enters will refer mainly to the region about San Francisco Bay. Here a quarter of the population of California is concentrated, and it is with their homes that I am especially concerned.

The style of the house is determined in no small degree by the material of which it is constructed, and this in turn is to a large measure regulated by cost or availability. Primitive people in many lands have found reeds, grasses, or leaves, thatched upon poles, the most readily obtainable material for making a shelter. Even in the rural districts of England the use of thatch may still be seen, but the danger of fire and the comparative instability of such work has caused it to be generally abandoned.

In all countries where forests of suitable timber are accessible, we find wooden houses predominate. Even such savages as the Thlingit Indians of Alaska and the New Zealand Maoris, both living in lands abundantly forested, abandoned the temporary huts of their ancestors for permanent houses of wooden slabs. In desert countries, on the contrary, where wood is scarce and difficult to obtain, we find the first evidences of the use of stone or clay for building purposes. The Pueblo Indians of Arizona, the Aztecs of Mexico and the early Egyptians are instances in point.

California is still in the period of wooden houses. With great forest areas unexploited and the modern facilities for converting trees into lumber, this is still by far the least expensive material available for building purposes. A brick house costs today nearly twice as much as a wooden house, and a structure of stone, or even of terra-cotta, is far more expensive than one of brick. Since the average home builder puts into his residence all he can afford, building of brick would mean to shrink the house to half its dimensions in wood. It therefore follows that brick and stone, for some time to come, will be available chiefly for public or commercial structures, except amongst the very rich, while the man of average means must be content with wood.

In this there is no hardship if the one essential rule be observed of using every material in the manner for which it is structurally best adapted, and of handling it in a dignified style. The failure to observe this rule is the great sin in most of the domestic architecture of America. A few illustrations will emphasize the point. The arch of masonry is the strongest structural use of stone or brick. An arch of wood, on the contrary, has no structural value, and is a mere imitation of a useful building form. It is generally painted to imitate the effect of stone, and thus sins even more seriously in becoming a sham. We feel that a woman with painted lips and cheeks is vulgar because she is shamming the beauty which only vigorous health can bestow ; so also is woodwork vulgar when it is covered over to imitate the architectural form of stone.

The rounded arch, although the most obvious type of faulty design in wood, is only one of many points in which the effect of stone construction is unwarrantably imitated in wood. The round tower, the curving bay window, and a multitude of detachable ornaments are cheaply rendered in wood when their very nature demands that they be built of masonry. It is a good general rule in timber construction to build in straight, angular lines, thus in a measure insuring the effect of strength, dignity, and repose.

Having determined the general form of construction in wood, it is next important to consider its right treatment and handling. Wood is a good material if left in the natural finish, but it is generally spoiled by the use of paint or varnish. This is a matter which perhaps cannot be entirely reasoned out. It must be seen and felt to be understood; and yet it is a point vital to artistic work. There is a refinement and character about natural wood which is entirely lost when the surface is altered by varnish and polish. Oil paint is the most deadly foe of an artistic wood treatment. It is hard and characterless, becoming dull and grimy with time and imparting a cold severity to the walls.

Wood is treated with paint for two avowed reasons — to protect it and to ornament it. Experience proves, however, that the protection afforded by paint is quite unnecessary in most climates. Shingles, if left to themselves, rot very slowly and in a very clean manner. Since the grain of the wood is in the direction of drainage, the rot is constantly washed out instead of accumulating. With painted clapboards, in which the grain runs crosswise to the drainage, on the contrary, dirt and grime are scrubbed into the wood, and a renewal of paint is necessary after a very few years.

Natural shingles last fully three times as long as a coat of paint, and are thus in the end an economy.

As to the second reason for treating wood with paint, ornamentation, let us consider for a moment wherein lies the beauty of a house. We are too prone to forget that a single house is but a detail in a landscape. In the country it is a mere incident amongst the trees or fields ; in the city it is but one of a street of houses. In either case its effect should never be considered apart from the whole. The exterior of a house should always be conceived so that it will harmonize with its surroundings. The safest means of effecting this is by leaving the natural material to the tender care of the elements. Wood in time weathers to a soft brown or gray in which the shadows are the chief marks of accent. The tones are sufficiently neutral to accord with any landscape, and the only criticism from an artistic point of view which can be made upon the coloring of such a group of houses is that they are rather sober and reserved. California has a remedy for this defect in the abundance of climbing flowers. Banksia rose, ivy-geranium, Wistaria, clematis, passion vine, Ampelopsis, and a joyous host of companion vines are ready to enliven any sober wall. Wire-mesh screens a foot from the house will protect the shingles from dampness, and our houses can thus be decked as for a carnival in a wealth of varying bloom.

A practice much in vogue of trimming shingle houses with white is especially to be deprecated since the white accent is utterly out of key with the rest of the house and attracts the attention out of all proportion to the importance of the parts thus emphasized. If color must be used, a creosote shingle stain for the roof, of dull red or a soft warm green, is not apt to destroy the color harmony of the house with reference to the surrounding landscape, but the difficulty is that crude harsh colors are so often chosen, or, if successfully avoided by the original colorist, may be applied by some less discriminating successor. The colors bestowed by nature always improve with time, and are therefore by far the safest.

Our consideration of the home has progressed only so far as the right use of one material. There are two other matters of fundamental importance, the style of architecture and the plan. Our discussion to this point would apply equally to any country or climate, but in the matters now to be treated, the environment must be reckoned with. A simple house need not, in an exact sense, be classed with any style of architecture, yet there are certain distinguishing features which seem to throw many of our recent homes into either the Classic, the Gothic, or the so-called "Mission" architecture of the Spanish.

With the California houses which pass under the name of "Colonial" I have no sympathy whatever. In the Eastern States the real colonial houses are genuinely beautiful and appropriate, set amidst green lawns and shadowed with venerable elms, but their charm lies more in the natural use of good materials than in the introduction of classic columns and other embellishments. The cheap imitations of such homes in California generally have no harmonious setting and are characterized by the use of inappropriate materials in an insincere way. I need instance but one example, that of a large wooden house painted red to suggest brick, with blocks of white trimming as a reminiscence of marble or granite. In this there is no attempt at deception, of course, but a mere copy of an effect produced by more expensive materials.

It is unnecessary to dwell at greater length on the inappropriateness of meaningless white-painted fluted columns of hollow wood, which support nothing worthy of their pretentiousness, of little balconies of turned posts, which are too small or inaccessible to be used, and many other vulgar accessories of ornament, made more glaring by a hard surface of white paint.

I therefore pass next to the Gothic house. A real problem here presents itself for serious consideration, one, in fact, concerning which our best architects are not fully in accord. In brief, the question is : Shall we bar the pointed roof from the valleys of California, and with it the Gothic spirit, on the ground that our climate does not demand it? Those who reply in the affirmative, point to the fact that we live in a land without snow, and that the steep-pitched roof is called for only as a means of shedding the heavy snow of a northern climate. They contend that since our climatic affinities are with the Mediterranean countries rather than with Germany, Britain, and Scandinavia, our architecture should follow the inspiration of the South rather than of the

North. Those who make this contention find their ideal in a masonry architecture with roofs of the slightest practicable pitch. I have much sympathy with this point of view, and yet the case does not seem quite so clear as some of its most consistent advocates conceive it. The problem seems to hinge, in part at least, on whether or not the steep-pitched roof is to be regarded only in the light of a snow-shed. If so, it is manifestly out of place in the valleys of Central and Southern California. But is there not another element involved in the pointed lines of Gothic architecture? Are the pinnacles and spires of a Gothic cathedral intended simply or mainly to carry off snow? It seems to me, on the contrary, that the whole pointed effect of Gothic archi-tecture is, in a measure at least, a means of expressing the ideal of aspiration. A flattened roof naturally carries the glance down to earth; a pointed roof, on the other hand, leads the eye upward to the sky. The two ideals are most completely embodied in the Greek temple and the Gothic cathedral, the one complete, finished, nobly crowning the earth, the other beautiful in itself but pointing heavenward toward spiritual things unrealized.

Even if the flatness of the Greek temple and the pointedness of the Gothic cathedral were primarily the result of the absence and presence of snow, these forms have, in the course of ages, become the embodiments of certain human ideals, the contented and the aspiring. The horizontal line suggests repose; the vertical line, action. If the Gothic spirit is to be introduced and perpetuated in

California, it will have a temperamental rather than a climatic rationale.

That the pointed roof is not an essential in a country with heavy winter snows is well exemplified by the Swiss chalet. Those who disparage the pointed roof most strongly as an importation from a land of snow are most ready to follow the type of house characteristic of Switzerland, where broad roofs of very slight pitch, supported by massive timbers, hold the snow to serve as a warm blanket.

If we turn to savage architecture to discover the natural genesis of roof lines, we find the Thlingit Indians in Alaska and the Maoris of southern New Zealand, both living in lands of winter snow, building houses with roof pitch but little steeper than that characteristic of Italy and Greece, while the Hawaiians, who dwell in the tropics and whose ancestors lived there in the remote past, build grass houses with roofs as steep as those of Norway. In the face of such unconscious testimony as to the lack of necessary relation between roof pitch and snow, I fail to see how any fair-minded student of architecture can continue to press the point.

Personally I have no wish to argue in favor of either roof pitch for California. It seems to me to be largely a matter of individual taste, to be determined by the preference of the builder for Gothic or Classic ideals. There is a practical advantage in the roof of low pitch, in that it gives an increase in attic room, but the steep roof, on the other hand, is a more perfect water-shed, and therefore less liable to leak.

RESIDENCE BY ERNEST COXHEAD. (DATE OF CONSTRUCTION UNKNOWN), BUILDING RECORDS SHOW THAT THE
HOUSE WAS LOCATED ON HEARST AVENUE. IT WAS DESTROYED IN THE BERKELEY FIRE OF 1923.

ALBERT SCHNEIDER HOUSE. BERNARD MAYBECK, ARCHITECT. 1907. PHOTOGRAPH COURTESY DOCUMENTS COLLECTION, COLLEGE OF ENVIRONMENTAL DESIGN, U.C. BERKELEY

The Mansard roof, with flat top enclosed with a railing, need not be discussed in this connection, since it is happily out of fashion and seems destined to remain so. Another form of flat roof — that characteristic of Egypt and Palestine — is, on the contrary, quite appropriate to California, and especially to city houses. In this style of architecture the outer walls of the house project above the roof level, enclosing an open-air garden on the house-top. Buildings thus designed are generally made of stone, brick, or plaster, although wood also may be fitly employed for a house of this description.

Our discussion of architectural styles has thus far been restricted to roof lines, and the conclusion reached is that taste and a feeling for simple, harmonious lines rather than climate is the governing principle in determining these. In the matter of windows, balconies, and the arrangement of the walls, on the contrary, climate plays an important rôle. Southern California is pre-eminently a land of sunshine, with slight rainfall, little fog, mild winters, and hot, dry summers. An out-of-door life is possible much of the year, and protection from the sun is a necessity to comfort. Deep recessed verandas, windows with deep reveals, and open rooms roofed over and with the sides protected by screens upon which vines may be trained, — all these are suitable to the climate of southern California, and to the sheltered valleys in the interior of the central part of the State. The Spanish architecture is especially appropriate in these regions. Heavy walls of masonry, secluded courts, outside corridors sheltered from the sun, and houses set flat upon the ground, are quite in keeping with a warm, arid country.

The region about San Francisco Bay has a very different climate. The proportion of sunny days is far less; during the winter there is an abundant rainfall, while in summer much foggy weather is experienced. The winters are so mild that furnace fires are seldom considered a necessity, while the summers are so cool that there are only a few days when sunlight is not welcome for its warmth. Thus it follows that about San Francisco Bay we need to introduce into our homes all the sunlight we can get. Here the deep shadowing porches or outside corridors are out of place, as are also deep-set windows of small dimensions. We need plenty of glass on the south, east and west. A small glass room on the south side of the house is a great luxury, as well as an economy in the matter of heating the entire home.

Furthermore, the bay climate is mild enough to enable people to sit out of doors during two-thirds of the year if shelter is provided against the prevailing sea breeze from the west. Wide porches without roofing, on the east side of the house, or on the south side with a wall of wood or glass at the western end, are therefore the best means of promoting an out-of-door life in the family. These porches are most useful when large enough to accommodate a table and chairs, and they may be protected from publicity by means of bamboo strip curtains or by a screen of vines. A

movable awning or a large Japanese umbrella overhead
makes the porch into a livable open-air room.

The lighting of the home is greatly improved by massing
the windows, thus avoiding the strain on the eyes occasioned by cross lights.   Three or four windows side by side
give a far better light than the same number scattered about
the room, and the wall space can be utilized to better advantage by this arrangement.   The old-fashioned hinged windows are more picturesque than the customary sort that slide
up and down with the aid of weights on pulleys concealed
between the walls; and leaded glass, when it can be
afforded, not only lends decorative effect to the house, but
also breaks up the view in a charming manner.

While insisting on abundant sunlight in homes about
San Francisco Bay, I cannot overlook the fascination of
wide eaves.   A house without eaves always seems to me
like a hat without a brim, or like a man who has lost his
eyebrows.   The decorative value of shadows cannot well be
overestimated ; and the problem thus becomes one of making
the most of the eaves without losing too much sunlight from
the rooms.   In this, so much depends on the location and
plan of the house that no general discussion would be of
much practical value.

The plan of the home, which, after all, is the great
factor in its convenience and livability, still remains for consideration.   If I were to make one suggestion only, it would
be to keep it large and simple in idea.   A generous living
room of ample dimensions is preferable to several small

rooms without distinctive character. The custom of having a front and back parlor is relegated to the limbo of our grandmothers, and in its stead one large living room suffices for family gatherings and the entertainment of friends. The dining-room may open off from this assembly room as an annex or alcove, closed with heavy curtains or with a large sliding door. Little surprises in the form of unexpected nooks or cabinets seen through long vistas, and other elements of mystery lend charm when done by an artist, but it is decidedly better for the inexpert to avoid all but the simplest and most natural expression.

A high ceiling, with its wide expanse of unused wall space, commonly gives a room a dreary effect which it is almost impossible to remove, although an extremely high ceiling, relieved by exposed rafters, is sometimes very charming, effectively revealing the roof as in a barn or chapel. In other respects the plan depends largely on the life of the family, in which sanitation, comfort, convenience and adaptability all must be well considered. No home is truly beautiful which is not fitted to the needs of those who dwell within its walls. A stairway upon which a tall man is in danger of bumping his head is an example of bad art. So, too, is a stairway with risers so high or a flight so long that the mother of the family will be over-fatigued in going up and down.

Too little attention is commonly paid to the interior finish. Anything that tends to emphasize the constructive quality of the work enhances its value. No ceiling ornament can

[30]

equal the charm of visible floor joists and girders, or of the rafters. They are not there merely to break up the monotony of a flat surface, but primarily to keep the upper stories from falling on our heads. Incidentally, they are a most effective decoration with their parallel lines and shadows. My own preference for the interior walls of a wooden house is wood. If an air space is left between the shingle wall and the inner lining, the house will not be too susceptible to changes of temperature without. It is only of late years that the full charm of the natural California redwood has been realized. Until recently it was treated with a stain and then varnished, but now this practice has given way to the use of surfaced wood, rubbed with a wax dressing to preserve the natural color, or left to darken without any preservative.

The redwood walls of the interior may be made by nailing vertical slabs to the outside of the studding, thus leaving the construction all exposed within, or by applying simple vertical panels to the inside of the studding. A very effective door is made of a single long, narrow panel of redwood, with the edges of the frame left square.

There are other satisfying interior finishes beside the natural planed redwood. An extremely interesting result can be obtained by taking rough-sawed boards or timbers, and slightly charring the surface. On rubbing this down with sand and an old broom, a soft brown color and an interesting wavy texture is produced. Redwood treated with sulphate of iron is turned a silver gray, like boards exposed for years to the weather, and gives an interesting color scheme to a room. Rough boards sawed and left without planing may be colored with a soft green creosote stain, which gives a peculiarly subdued and mossy effect. Other stains, or even the application of Dutch leaf metal or of gold paint on wood, may be used with caution by an experienced artist, but should be avoided by the novice. Planks or beams, surfaced with the adze, have a fascinating texture, this finish being especially effective for exposed rafters.

A hard pine flooring answers very well in an inexpensive house, although a harder wood is to be preferred if it can be afforded. A coating of white shellac, followed by weekly polishings with wax and a friction brush, leaves the floor in good order.

I have thus far said nothing of ornament in describing the construction of the home. It is far better to have no ornament than to have it either badly designed or wrongly placed. We sometimes see shingle houses with a square piece of machine carving of commonplace design to relieve the monotony of a plain wall surface. The bare wall would have been inoffensive, but the ornament spoils the simplicity and effectiveness of the entire house. Ornament should grow out of the construction, and should always be an individual expression adapted to the particular space it is to fill. Thus all machine-turned moldings, sawed-out brackets, or other mechanical devices for ornament, may well be rigorously excluded.

As the life of the home centers about the fireplace, this

may appropriately be the most beautiful feature of a room. Let its ornamentation be wholly individual and hand wrought. Carved corbels, supporting a plain shelf, or some good conventional form done in terra-cotta or tiling, may be used to advantage; but if something cannot be made for that particular spot, be content with a good, generous fireplace of the rough, richly colored clinker brick or of pressed brick, or big tiles. If good in form, the hearth will be a beautiful corner, full of good cheer.

While on the subject of ornament, I cannot refrain from a word on the lack of vitality in the decorative work of even our best architects. This is due to the fact that instead of making designs from the decorative forms of animals and plants about them, they almost invariably copy, with more or less exactness, the designs from architectural works of Europe. How much easier to take books of details of Italian chapels and Greek temples, than to go to that wonderful book of nature and create from her treasure-house new motives! But until the latter method is followed, decorative work will be feeble and imitative.

Thus far our discussion has been confined to houses built, within and without, of wood. An outer covering of bricks may be substituted for the shingles without materially altering the design in other respects, and, if the construction be sufficiently massive to warrant it, slate or tile may replace the shingles of the roof, making the whole more durable and substantial in effect. But it is a mistake to suppose that a wooden structure is necessarily perishable in its nature. I am told that there are such houses in good preservation in Continental Europe which antedate Columbus, and we all know of the Anne Hathaway cottage and other Shakespearean relics of Stratford.

The wooden house may be varied by the use of plaster, either on the exterior or the interior. The point to be emphasized is never to use plaster with wood as if the construction were of masonry. The only safeguard is to show the construction. Houses built in the old English style, with exposed timbers between the plaster, are very picturesque. It has been ascertained that plaster applied to wooden laths will soon fall off, but when expanded metal is used as a foundation, the plaster seems to stand indefinitely. It may be toned to some soft, warm shade with a permanent water-color paint.

There is another type of plaster house much in vogue in California which is to be condemned as an unmitigated sham. This is the style which masks under the name of "Mission" architecture, and which imitates the externals of the work of the old Spanish missionaries while missing every vital element in their buildings. The modern structure in Mission style is built of wood, either completely covered with plaster or with exposed wood painted to imitate it. Many features of masonry construction, such as round pillars covered with stucco, arches and circular windows, are introduced. The construction is generally slight, but with a massive external appearance, and the roofing in most cases is of tin tiles painted red. Such work as this will do

NEW ZEALAND MAORI HOUSE SHOWING ROOF OF MODERATE PITCH.

HAWAIIAN HOUSE SHOWING STEEP-PITCHED ROOF.

well enough for a world's fair, which is confessedly but a fleeting show, but it is utterly unworthy as the home of any honest man.

The Spanish missionaries did their work in adobe, brick, tile and stone. Much of it was covered with plaster and whitewashed. The charm of the low, simple buildings surrounding a court, with corridors supported by arches extending both on the outside and inside, can only be realized by one who has studied the lovely ruins of the Spanish occupation, or better still, by one who has visited Spanish countries. The glare of the whitewashed walls is relieved by the deep shadows of the sheltering corridors or porch roofs, the soft red tiles crown the work, and vines and orchards, with fountains and palm trees in the court, make a beautifully harmonious setting. There is a romantic charm about such architecture and an historic association which California needs to cherish, but to mimic it with cheap imitations in wood is unworthy of us. If we are unwilling to take the pains, or if we cannot afford to do the work genuinely, let us not attempt it. We may carry out the general form in wood if we choose, but let it then be frankly a wooden house, or a structure of wood and plaster worked out constructively as such. Furthermore, as I have already pointed out, the climate of San Francisco Bay, with its large percentage of cloudy days, is not suited to deep recessed porches that cut the sun from the first story.

The use of plaster as an interior finish has been, until the last few years in California, so much a matter of course that I should have mentioned it first were it not that I wished to emphasize the superiority of the natural wood interior for a wooden house. If plaster is used, however, let it be with visible rafters. It may be toned or papered in any soft, warm shade, but the use of a mechanically printed wall-paper I should avoid under any and all circumstances. As this is a matter which concerns the furnishing of the home more especially, a fuller discussion of the point may be reserved for the following chapter.

If it seems to any that too much of this discussion has been devoted to wood construction, my answer has already been given — namely, that most people cannot afford, at the present day, to build of any other material, and that consequently a full consideration of the principles governing the right use of wood is a matter of the greatest immediate importance. At the same time, it is well to point out that every advance in the building of masonry homes is a progressive step, since it makes for greater stability, lessens the danger of fire, and saves our forests, which are so needful to the prosperity of the State. In masonry architecture the same fundamental idea should prevail, of using the material in the manner which emphasizes its strength and constructive value. Ornament should be studied with the same care and used with the same restraint as in wood.

Now for a last word on home building : Let the work be simple and genuine, with due regard to right proportion and harmony of color ; let it be an individual expression of the life which it is to environ, conceived with loving care for the uses of the family. Eliminate in so far as possible all factory-made accessories in order that your dwelling may not be typical of American commercial supremacy, but rather of your own fondness for things that have been created as a response to your love of that which is good and simple and fit for daily companionship. Far better that our surroundings be rough and crude in detail, provided that they are a vital expression conceived as part of an harmonious scheme, than that they be finished with mechanical precision and lacking in genuine character. Beware the gloss that covers over a sham !

THE FURNISHING OF THE HOME

WHEN the home is built, it must be occupied. It is to be used, lived in, made a part and expression of a family circle. First of all, it must be furnished, and the taste and thought revealed in this task determines in no small degree the character it will assume and impress upon its occupants. It is therefore of the first importance that the furnishing be done deliberately, step by step, piece by piece, so that it becomes a growth and expression of the interests and ideals of the family. The thoughts that I have endeavored to make clear concerning the building of the home apply equally to its furnishing. Simplicity, significance, utility, harmony — these are the watchwords!

Although the furnishment may better be a matter of deliberate growth rather than of immediate completion, it by no means follows that the work should be haphazard and without plan. On the contrary, just as the painter in creating a picture may not know in advance all the details and subtleties which he is to embody, but nevertheless has his general composition and color scheme well in mind, so should he who fits out a room consider in advance the underlying idea of tone and form. The first object is to create an atmosphere. How often we enter an apartment, full of elegant and beautiful things, in which there is no continuity of idea, no central thought which dominates the place! And when we come upon some simple room about which there is a sense of rest and harmony, we do not always stop to analyze the effect to see how it is produced. We feel that there is an intangible idea back of all the detail, and it pleases us, although we know not why.

As a rule it will be found that the harmony of an apartment is determined by its color scheme. An illustration of a gross violation will serve to enforce the point. If the window curtains were of so *bizarre* and unassorted a character that upon each window hung a drapery of a different color, some figured, some striped and others plain, even the most unobservant eye would detect that the room looked absurdly ill furnished. Upon the substitution, for this motley array of curtains, of some warm, quiet fabric without ornamentation, an appearance of harmony would at once seem dawning upon the room. But if the walls were of white plaster or of some crude figured wall-paper, the desired unity would be but dimly felt. What a change is wrought by covering the entire wall-space with a good warm color, either in harmony with or in judicious contrast to the curtains! It is the background of the picture, the dominant note of the chord, the underlying idea of the room, which needs only elaboration and accent to produce a finished whole.

This matter of color scheme is so fundamental to any successful results in furnishing that it may be well to consider a little more in detail what colors to use and what to avoid.

No definite and final rules can be formulated on this subject, for in the last analysis taste is the only guide. In general, however, I should begin by excluding white. A large mass of white on the walls makes a glare which is extremely fatiguing to the eyes. The light is too diffused and is far more trying than a blaze of sunlight streaming through a mass of windows. A similar effect may be noted out of doors upon a hazy day when the sun is but thinly veiled behind a white mist. On such occasions the glare is positively painful. While a large mass of white is thus to be avoided for physiological reasons, even a small spot of it will often be objectionable from an artistic point of view. The eye as it ranges freely about the room is unduly arrested by the bit of white which fails to fit into its proper relation with the whole. How seldom does a painter venture to use untoned white in a picture, and how carefully he leads up to it when he does introduce it! The same principle applies to the color scheme of a room. A picture surrounded by a white mat stands out of all relation to the environing walls. Indeed, I should use white as part of a decorative scheme only where the idea of great cleanliness needs emphasis, or in making a human figure the culminating note in the home picture. A white spread for the dinner table, setting off the glint of silver and cut-glass or the color of patterned dishes, has an appropriateness all its own, especially when the room is artificially lighted. For breakfast and lunch, during the daylight hours, the bare wood table, with dishes upon mats, always seems to me more attractive.

The next guiding thought, although any such may have
its exceptions, is that cold colors are to be avoided and
warm tones used instead. Pale blues, grays or greens are
not as a rule cheerful, while buff, brown and red, or occasionally deep blue or rich green, are full of warmth and
brightness. It is always safe to be conservative in the background color, and a neutral tone is therefore preferable to a
color aggressively pronounced.

It will now be apparent why a wood interior is so satisfactory. The color of the natural wood, and especially of
redwood, makes a warm, rich and yet sufficiently neutral
background for the furniture. Some of our lighter woods,
notably pine and cedar, may be stained or burned to a dark
tone as already specified in the preceding chapter, provided
that no glazed surface be put upon them with varnish or
polish. A slightly irregular texture is more interesting on
a wall than an absolutely uniform finish. Natural wood with
its varied graining is one of the most charmingly modulated
surfaces. Painted burlap glued to the wall makes an attractive finish on account of its coarse, irregular weave. Japanese grass-cloth has a similar interest, and is very effective
in combination with gilding. I know of a plaster ceiling
painted with liquid gold which is beautifully harmonious and
elegant in combination with redwood paneled walls. Rough
plaster may be toned with calcimine to any appropriate
shade, while smooth plaster is better when covered with
cartridge paper or with some plain fabric.

Although many architects of admirable taste may not

agree, I venture to suggest the elimination of figured wall-paper, and indeed of all machine-figured work about the home. Most papers are undeniably bad ; a few are equally undeniably beautiful in design. But if the contention for which I am standing has any weight—namely, that ornament should be used with reserve and be studied for the particular space it is to fill—then even an unquestionably good wall-paper is inappropriate for three reasons,—because the ornament is used too lavishly and indiscriminately, be-cause it cannot be turned out by machinery suited to the particular wall upon which it is to be imposed, and, further-more, because it detracts from any ornament which may be put next it. A picture or a vase, for instance, is never so effective when placed against a patterned background as when surrounded by a plain tone of appropriate color.

But enough of walls and surfaces ! Let us assume that a good color has been secured and in a soft, unobtrusive texture. Attention may next be given to the draperies. Many people insist on window shades that shoot up and down on rollers—smooth, opaque, characterless things that give a stiffness and mechanical rigidity to the windows. Curtains hung by brass rings upon rods are all-sufficient to cut out the sun by day and to exclude the view of out-siders by night, and they are far more graceful and soft in effect. The only difficulty is to get material that will not fade when left in the steady glare of the sun. All the so-called art denims and burlaps with which I have had experi-ence are so badly dyed that a very short exposure bleaches them beyond recognition, but the coarse dark blue Chinese denim is very serviceable. The satin-finish burlap, undyed, is also satisfactory on account of its permanence. Linen crash of an ecru color, Japanese grass-cloth, and some coarse, simple ecru nets are most effective. Curtains made of fine strips of bamboo lashed together give a soft, pleasing light in the room, but do not completely cut out the sun. They may be used to great advantage in combination with some heavier material, such as colored ticking or corduroy. Soft leather in the natural tan makes elegant and substantial curtains, but is rather expensive. Pongee is good, although, like all silks, it rots after long exposure to the sun.

In addition to window curtains, portières are often useful draperies, for giving privacy to an alcove, or between apartments where a door is unnecessary. Oriental hangings, such as Bagdad curtains, if made with the old dyes, are especially effective, but a plain chenille curtain, or even one of such coarser material as burlap, is always safe if its color harmonizes with the room. When hand-made Oriental hangings cannot be afforded and some ornament is desired, a conventional decoration in gold cord can be stitched to the border, or a little color, preferably in dark rich tones, may be cautiously added in embroidery or appliqué.

I assume that the floor of our home be of natural wood, shellaced and waxed, and afterwards polished with a friction brush. Cleanliness, if not an æsthetic impulse, should prompt this. One or two fine Oriental rugs — Bokharas, Cashmeres, or Persians, for example — made with the old dyes, are a great addition to any room, but a rag carpet serves as a passable substitute. It will hardly be necessary after all that has been said about machine ornament, to urge the exclusion of all modern patterned rugs and carpets. These are generally characterized by hard, set designs, mechanically precise, made in crude colors that fade ere long to sorry-looking tones. Better far is a piece of plain Brussels carpet of good color.

Having attended to the background, and the window curtains, portières and rugs in harmonizing tones, with here and there a note of accent or of contrast, if this be skilfully managed, the atmosphere of the room is established. It now remains to introduce the furniture. Much of this can be built in to the special places designed for it. Still the restraint in ornament should be kept steadily in mind. The first essential of the furniture is good, simple design and thorough-going workmanship,—no veneer, no paint or varnish, no decorations stuck on to give the piece a finish, but plain, honest, straightforward work !

The kinds of furniture which most readily lend themselves to being built permanently into the house are window- and fireplace-seats, book-shelves, and sideboards. The seats can be made quite plain, and if hinged serve the additional purpose of store chests. Book-shelves call for little or no ornament, although the end boards may be massive and carved if desired. There is much opportunity for making the sideboard picturesque, with paneled or leaded-glass doors, attached with ornamental strap hinges of

GLIMPSE OF A SPANISH CALIFORNIA MISSION.

GEORGE H. BOKE HOUSE, ARCHITECT BERNARD MAYBECK, 1902. WELL-MAINTAINED TODAY ON PANORAMIC WAY.

wrought iron or hammered brass. The arrangement of shelves and cupboards in a sideboard gives great scope for effective design.

With such pieces built in, and with a good tone to the rooms accented by rugs, portières and curtains, the home begins to assume a furnished aspect, and it is easy now to see what is needed and what will harmonize. Furniture made to order by a cabinet-maker, or even by a good carpenter, will be found of especial interest if simple models are followed. In the furniture as in the house itself it is well to emphasize the construction. Panels held together with double dove-tailed blocks, joints secured with pegs, and tenons let through mortises and held with wedges, are always evidences of good honest workmanship.

As to the design of such furniture, straight lines expressing the construction and utility in the most natural manner are safest, and only an experienced artist can safely deviate from such. There are a few exceptions, however, which are not only justifiable but often desirable. A round top for a dining-table is very pleasing on account of the feeling of equality of all who sit about it. It seems in a way more sociable than a table with a head and foot. A small square table can be made with two or more round tops of different sizes which fit down upon it, to be used as occasion requires. While a chair with square legs is massive and dignified in effect, the rounded legs give lightness and grace. A light and very inexpensive chair which might well be in more general use in California is the simple form made with strips of rawhide for a seat. It is a relic of the mission days, I believe, and is thoroughly appropriate to the style of house we are contemplating. Rush-bottom square-post chairs are substantial, comfortable and most harmonious in the simple room. A chair with the seat sloping backward and with the back at right angles to the seat is more comfortable than one with the seat parallel to the floor, which makes one sit bolt upright. Italian chairs carved of black walnut have a grace and elegance that give a touch of luxury to the most unpretentious home.

It would be possible to consider furniture in endless detail, but my object is rather to get at certain principles and ideals that will form a basis for working out the *minutiæ* according to individual taste. The chest is a good old-fashioned piece of furniture that may well be revived. Any good, well-made hinged boxes, and especially those of white cedar and the Chinese camphor-wood chests, are useful and attractive. The Chinese chests are covered with an ugly varnish which can be removed with strong lye, carefully rubbed on with a stout swab. Chests covered with leather and bound in brass are very elegant when they can be afforded. Wood-boxes near the fireplace may be left plain, or stained, carved or burned in ornamental designs. In a large room screens can be used to advantage. They may be made of big simple panels of wood, or of leather, either plain or ornamented with burning and coloring.

Chinese teak-wood furniture is generally good in design and may be had very richly carved. Old-fashioned mahogany bedsteads, bureaus and chairs are often beautifully simple in their lines and appropriate to the setting I have endeavored to picture. Oak furniture is now obtainable made in the "old mission" style, which is so good in form and workmanship that it leaves nothing to be desired.

The various handicrafts are brought into play in the furnishing of the home. Metal work is as indispensable as wood work, and again the same general principles should govern selection — good work, good form, simple design. The plainest are the safest. Locks, catches and fixtures of black iron, or of solid brass without ornament, are sure to be unobjectionable. The andirons may also be plain, or they may be ornamented as richly as taste suggests, provided the work be hand-wrought.

I have often been asked if the use of electric lights in a house which thus emphasizes the handicrafts was not out of harmony with the spirit of the place. Personally, I am fond of candles in brass, bronze or silver candlesticks, but the light is neither strong nor steady enough to satisfy the practical needs. I have found the pleasantest results in lighting to be attained by the use of electric lights subdued by lanterns. If the electric bulbs are suspended some six or eight inches from the wall on brackets, they may hang as low as desired without being in the way. Various types of Chinese, Japanese and Moorish lanterns can be found which give a soft, pleasing light and are very decorative. Old brass and bronze lanterns are the most beautiful, but many simpler and less costly substitutes will be discovered by those who search in our Oriental bazaars. Good lamps with artistic shades are hard to find, but there is an improvement in these to be noted which promises better things ere long. Covers for gas and oil-stoves made of sheet brass riveted into cylinders and ornamented according to the skill and ingenuity of the maker would be a most acceptable addition to our furniture.

To write of vases and other pottery would call for one or more separate chapters, but a hint or two may not be out of place. At the risk of repetition I would say again that unless the ornament be unquestionably fine, do with none at all. Chinese ginger jars, earthenware pots, Italian wine flasks with straw casings, are all better than showy vases that are not good in color, form or workmanship. The Japanese and Chinese are the master potters, and if the detestable stuff which they manufacture for the American trade be eliminated, their work is generally good and often exquisitely beautiful. Much excellent pottery is now made in our own country, and the number of genuinely refined and simple wares is constantly increasing, showing a gradual elevation of taste among our people.

Of other useful ornaments may be mentioned bellows, South Sea Island fans, baskets, especially those of our own misused Indians, and hanging Japanese baskets for plants. Potted plants add a touch of life and color which cannot be otherwise given to a room. Masses of books have an ornamental value which is heightened by the idea of culture of which they are the embodiment.

It remains now to consider only the purely non-utilitarian ornament — statues, pictures and wall decorations. Since most dwellers in simple homes cannot afford great works of art, they must enjoy these in museums, and for their homes content themselves with reproductions. Plaster casts toned to a soft creamy shade and surfaced with wax are, if well chosen, a most effective form of ornament.

The pictures a man selects to hang upon his wall are a perpetual witness of his degree of culture. They are ever present as an unconscious factor in shaping our lives and thought. They serve no useful purpose and have no meaning except as they bring before us something of the ideal. The test of a good picture is its inexhaustible quality, both of form and of content ; but time alone can make this test. When the work of a master has been handed down through centuries, when it has been copied and scrutinized and criticized by generations and still holds its place, we may be sure that it contains something that will enrich our lives. If the world has lived with it for ages, it needs must profit us to dwell in its sight. We cannot have the original picture, but a photograph giving all but its color may be obtained for a mere trifle. Thus our walls may be graced with the thought of Botticelli, Leonardo, Raphael and Michael Angelo, just as readily as with the commonplace work that so often passes current for genuine art. When we have lived with the masters for years, and have absorbed their message, then we may trust ourselves to test the work of the moderns in the light of the insight we have gained from their predecessors.

It may be urged that we want color on our walls, and that tinted casts and photographs of the masterpieces fail to give this. In vain I point to the Oriental rugs, the colored curtains, the green of the potted plants — still the demand for colored pictures must be satisfied, and this without great cost. If one really loves form and color for themselves, I know of but one means of satisfying this adequately and inexpensively. Japanese prints are seldom great in idea, and they therefore miss the highest quality of art expression, but for delicacy and subtlety of coloring and grace of form they are unexcelled. A few prints selected with discrimination and simply framed will give just the touch of accidental color which the room seems to require.

California has harbored a number of painters of exceptional ability, and those who can afford original paintings by our best local artists need not go abroad for their pictures. America has produced but one Keith, and his work has been done in San Francisco.

Many of our artists are now looking toward decorative work as a field of activity, instead of confining their attention to easel pictures, and this is a most wholesome change. A decorative frieze or a set piece designed to occupy a given space in a room, and conceived in harmony with its setting, is apt to be far more effective than a number of small detached pictures scattered at random about the walls.

A word on framing pictures and our cursory survey of house furnishing must come to an end. The old-fashioned idea seemed to be that a picture was merely an excuse for

displaying an elaborate frame. Now people have come to
realize that the frame is nothing but the border of the picture. Here again a simple form is always safe. A plain,
finely finished surface without ornamentation is never out of
place. In choosing the color of a frame, the middle tone
of the picture is the best guide. Thus in framing a brown
photograph, a brown mat intermediate in tone between the
high lights and the deepest shadows will probably be found
most effective. The wood is least obtrusive if toned to
match the mat or just a shade darker. Photographs look
well framed in wood without a mat, but with a fine line of
gold next the picture. Gold frames are scarcely in keeping
with a simple home, but if used should be of the finest
workmanship and the most chaste design. They are, as
a rule, inappropriate except on oil paintings, although a gold
mat with simple gold border occasionally looks well on a
water-color.

I know it is not safe to lay down the law where matters
of taste are involved, but my excuse must be that it is better
to convey a definite impression, even though it be a narrow
one, rather than to be so broad that all concreteness vanishes
in glittering generalities. Many types of homes may be
good and beautiful which do not come within the compass of
this sketch. I have tried only to give some tangible expression of my own conception of the simple home, trusting that
the practical hints embodied may be the means of showing
some people who have felt the need of more artistic surroundings a tolerably secure means of attaining them.

[51]

HOME LIFE

THE very planning, building, and furnishing of such a home as I have endeavored to describe will prove a powerful incentive toward a simpler and more significant family life. Take the one item of pictures, for example. If the selection of these involves a preliminary study of the history of art, and an acquaintance with the aims and ideals of the great masters, what a step in culture will have been achieved! And in surroundings of simple dignity, light and flippant music will soon appear vulgar and inopportune. Ephemeral ragtime airs will yield precedence to Schumann and Chopin, to Beethoven and Bach. Poetry will be in keeping with the spirit of such a home, and Keats and Shelley will not be forgotten.

A superficial liking for æsthetic things may be accompanied with the most trifling of dilettantism, and have no effect in deepening spiritual life, but a real understanding or even a resolute effort to understand and sympathize with the ideal of beauty must of necessity strengthen and enrich the soul of man. Gradually the dweller in the simple home will come to ponder upon the meaning of art, and will awaken to that illuminating insight that *all art is a form of service inspired by love.* It will then become apparent how truly the home is the real art center. The great Christian painters have chosen for the theme of their noblest works

LIBRARY AS IT WAS DURING KEELER'S RESIDENCE AT HIGHLAND PLACE HOUSE FROM 1895-1907. BERNARD MAY-BECK ARCHITECT, 1895. ALTHOUGH THE ROOFLINES AND GENERAL STRUCTURE HAVE NOT BEEN ALTERED, THE PRESENT STUCCOED HOUSE IS MORE A PRODUCT OF MAYBECK'S EXTENSIVE REMODELING IN 1920

BERNARD MAYBECK RESIDENCE, BERNARD MAYBECK ARCHITECT (1892-1902), DIVIDED INTO APARTMENTS AND COVERED WITH ASBESTOS SIDING, THIS FIRST HOUSE OF MAYBECK'S STILL STANDS, UNRECOGNIZABLY ALTERED. GROVE AND BERRYMAN STREETS.

the divine mother looking with adoration upon her child. And what mother has not the halo of divinity about her as she bends with loving solicitude above the helpless life that is to be made or marred by the power she exercises over it. We hear much in these days of race suicide, but the menace comes not from those who love their homes. It is only amongst those for whom the feverish pleasures of the world outweigh the simple joys of the hearthstone that this danger exists.

In the thought of service lies the salvation of the race as of the individual, and in the simple home, service comes so naturally. Service is love realized in activity. The very mark which distinguishes love from lust is this same service — this willingness to objectify faith in work, to share tasks, to lighten the burdens of another. As love is the end of life, so is service the test and sign of love.

What is the home but a temple consecrated to love, where the form of worship is service? And the woman is the high priestess, the one who makes the supreme sacrifice, the one who has the supreme reward. The idea of woman's rights becomes insignificant in the face of this great privilege of service. But the woman must be fitted for the service — the higher the service the more complete the training. Higher education is a matter of course for the woman of whom we are to expect higher service. And what higher service does life afford than the molding of the plastic mind of the child, the expanding of the soul's horizon, the developing of character, the leading, by precept and example, of the human spirit up the height of Sinai where it may stand in the presence of its God.

Not alone in the relation of parents to offspring, but in all the associations of family life is this touchstone of service illuminating. The relations of children to one another and to the home are exalted by it. The duties of the servant are no longer those of a drudge when elevated to the dignity of participation in family service and in the advancement and joy of home life. And the mistress also has a duty of service toward her helper which is not discharged by the payment of certain sums of money — a duty to aid in lightening the tasks, in making the work more rational, more interesting, more orderly, and in making the leisure more joyous, more profitable toward attaining the ends of refinement and humanity.

Of all reforms needed in the life of the home, that of the relation of the man to his family is most pressing. Modern materialism demands of far too many men an unworthy sacrifice. That the wife and children may live in ostentation the man must be a slave to business, rushing and jostling with the crowd in the scramble for wealth. A simpler standard of living will give him more time for art and culture, more time for his family, more time to live.

The day is ripe for the general adoption of this idea of the simple home. People are growing weary of shams and are longing for reality. They will never get it till they learn that the ideal is the real, that beauty is truth, and that love is the inspiration for beauty. Let those who would see a higher culture in California, a deeper life, a nobler humanity, work for the adoption of the simple home among all classes of people, trusting that the inspiration of its mute walls will be a ceaseless challenge to all who dwell within their shadow, for beauty and character.